Vera Lex

Journal of the International Natural Law Society

Copyright © 2010
Pace University Press
1 Pace Plaza
New York, NY 10038

ISBN 1-935625-07-1
ISBN-13 978-1-935625-07-0
ISSN 0893-4851

Contributors
Address all submissions and correspondence to The Editor, VERA LEX, Pace University, Department of Philosophy & Religious Studies, 1 Pace Plaza, New York, NY 10038. Please send two copies of the paper submitted. Include adequate margins, double space everything (text, notes, works cited, quotations). Use U.S. spelling and punctuation style, (e.g. periods inside quotation marks; "double quotes" for opening and closing quotations). The University of Chicago Manual of Style, is to be consulted regarding matters of style. Notes are to be numbered consecutively (in Arabic numerals) and placed at the bottom of the page.

Subscribers
VERA LEX is published annually by Pace University Press, 41 Park Row, Room 1510, New York, NY 10038. Subscription price: $40. Please send all subscription inquiries to: PaceUP@pace.edu

Indexing and Abstracting
VERA LEX is indexed in Philosopher's Index.
Copyright © 2010 by Pace University Press. Permission is required to reprint an article or part of an article.

VERA LEX, the journal of the International Natural Law Society, was established to communicate and dialogue on the subject of natural law and natural right, to introduce natural law philosophy into the mainstream of contemporary thought, and to strengthen the current revived interest in the discussion of morals and law and advance its historical research.

Harold Brown
Editor
Richard Connerney
Contributing Editor
Virginia Black & Robert Chapman
Editors Emeriti

Editorial Board

Gregory Kerr
Department of Philosophy & Theology, DeSales University
John Krummel
Department of Religion, Temple University
Eddis Miller
Pace University Department of Philosophy & Religious Studies
Alice Ramos
Department of Philosophy, St. John's University
Lisa Sideris
Department of Religious Studies, Indiana University
Peter Widulski
Loyola University School of Law, New Orleans

Why do we use a shell (*Nautilus pomplilus Linnaeus*) to symbolize vera lex? The logarithmic spiraling and overlapping chambers of the shell are endless. They suggest a patterned development and evolution that, by its radial and circular design, never comes to an end. This means that the shell is at once specific and real, while its form, like law, is abstract and ideal.

The pattern of a shell is, like good law, uniform, regular and reliable. It can therefore be anticipated and known. The pattern of a shell is balanced, like justice. Una iustitia.

A shell is a biological being. Like law, it has life and dynamic. It grows. (There is an average of thirty growth lines per chamber, one for every day in the lunar cycle, suggesting that a new chamber is put down each lunar month and a new growth line each day, thus recording two different natural rhythms, lunar and solar.)

The shell is a universal and common object known to everyone. A shell is not soft tissue easily destroyed. And yet, like liberty, it is fragile in certain respects if stepped on with an iron boot. It has to be guarded with vigilance or it is crushed.

In every shell lives a nautilus. If the shell is law, the nautilus (snail) is a person—it is alive—person and law. Their destinies, like person and law, are interdependent.

Vera Lex

leges innumerae, una iustitia

CONTENTS

NEW SERIES VOLUME 11, NUMBERS 1&2 **WINTER 2010**

FEATURED ARTICLES

On the Alleged Disintegration of Natural Law Theory	John J. Liptay, Jr.	1
Let's Skill All the Lawyers: Shakespearean Lessons on the Nature of Law	Harold Anthony Lloyd	33
Honor, Dignity and the *Summum Bonum:* Kant's Retributivism in Context	Jacob M. Held	75
Mencius: Plato with a Country on His Side. Looking to China for Help with Jurisprudential Problems	Seth Gurgel	101
Nietzsche, Natural Law and the Reshaping of *Physis*	Yunus Tuncel	129

BOOK REVIEWS

Fundamentalism: The Search for Meaning by Malise Ruthven	Peter P. Cvek	145
The Bourgeois Virtues by Deirdre McCloskey	Richard Connerney	151
Contributors		156

FEATURED ARTICLES

ON THE ALLEGED DISINTEGRATION OF NATURAL LAW THEORY
John J. Liptay, Jr.

Pauline Westerman's study, *The Disintegration of Natural Law Theory: Aquinas to Finnis*,[1] poses a serious challenge to those working in the area of natural law theory that has yet to be answered. In a detailed and wide-ranging treatment of several of the tradition's seminal thinkers, Westerman aims to make the case that natural law theory has, in effect, run its course, and explicitly rejects the view, expounded most rigorously and influentially by John Finnis and his associates, that the natural law tradition can be developed and restated by appeal to the conceptual framework of Thomas Aquinas. Instead, she argues that Aquinas' writings have sown the seeds for natural law theory's demise, such that the numerous and various reformulations of natural law can be read as a long story of decline. An understanding and estimation of the value of Aquinas' account of natural law thus underlies both the claim that natural law can be articulated and developed as a compelling moral and legal theory and Westerman's belief that intractable difficulties intrinsic to any account of natural law lead to the theory's disintegration. Such a state of affairs invites further inquiry and an effort at resolution. I therefore propose (I) to examine Westerman's reading of Aquinas and the problems inherent in his account that she identifies, and (II) to argue that her findings are damaging neither to Aquinas' own natural law theory nor to the prospects of natural law theory generally. Indeed, Westerman's "problems" can be set aside through a more accurate interpretation and more comprehensive reading of Aquinas' text, a better understanding of what moral philosophy can and cannot do, and a denial of her claim that the subsequent development

[1] Pauline C. Westerman, *The Disintegration of Natural Law Theory: Aquinas to Finnis* (Leiden: Brill, 1998), hereafter cited in text as *DNLT*.

of Aquinas' account involved a "forced move" in consequence of its deficiencies. As such, her work does not require one to abandon the project of solidifying, developing, and applying natural law theory.

I. WESTERMAN'S PROJECT: MAKING THE CASE FOR NATURAL LAW'S DISINTEGRATION

Since Westerman's assessment of Aquinas' natural law theory is based on a general overview of his account, it is necessary to come to grips with her reading of Aquinas on a range of issues and to clarify her aims and methodology.

Two basic strategies can be deployed to oppose the claims of a particular theory of natural law. One can either show that the principles and precepts constitutive of a particular account of natural law cannot be considered true, or establish the truth of an alternative set of normative propositions.[2] Westerman's approach to natural law theory is unique in that she does not proceed in either of these ways. While she is convinced that natural law is not something "real" (*DNLT*, 12), she does not argue the point or that one should adopt a different set of general foundational principles. What she sets out to prove is that a consideration of the history of natural law theory should lead one to abandon the search for such foundational principles in the realms of law and morality insofar as they are of no assistance when it comes to making practical determinations. Moral and legal reflection should take their starting points from those concepts that are actually used to make such determinations, instead of from natural law theory.

In this way Westerman's work is proposed as a direct challenge to Finnis' understanding of the natural law tradition.[3] For Finnis

---

[2] John Finnis, "Introduction," in *Natural Law*, ed. John Finnis (Dartmouth: Aldershot, 1991), 1: xi-xxiii at xi.

[3] This, in part, accounts for the heavy reliance on Finnis' works throughout this paper. But I also share William E. May's judgment that "[p]erhaps the finest presentation of St. Thomas' moral thought is to be found in John Finnis, *Aquinas: Moral, Political, and Legal Theory* (Oxford: Oxford University Press, 1998), chapters II-V, pp. 20-186—and, indeed, in his numerous other studies as well. See William E. May, *Catholic Bioethics and the Gift*

develops a number of foundational elements of Aquinas' account, indicates how they can be used to order and guide choices and actions and in the creation and formation of laws, and argues that they were transformed and undermined by subsequent natural law thinkers (*DNLT*, 2). Westerman faults Finnis, however, for failing to advance a sufficiently detailed criticism of the developments of the tradition to which he objects, and for her part advances a different understanding of that tradition. In her view, subsequent developments of the natural law tradition are not to be understood as distortions of Aquinas' account, but "as rational attempts to solve certain problems inherent in the theoretical framework which was handed to them" (*DNLT*, 6). Even if she at times speaks of the "solid foundations" of Aquinas' account (*DNLT*, 6), Westerman's view is that Aquinas' doctrine of natural law is compromised by insoluble difficulties and, as such, cannot be relied on or returned to as a point of departure for the development of a coherent and robust natural law theory which can be used to make concrete moral and legal determinations. And though Aquinas' successors should not be understood as distorting his account, in the development of the tradition the number of intractable difficulties has only increased, rendering *any* version of natural law theory an inappropriate or unsuitable guide for moral and legal reflection.

Westerman's study appropriately begins, then, with a treatment of Aquinas' doctrine of natural law, as this has the most relevance for contemporary accounts (*DNLT*, 13-14). But, in addition, she investigates the theories of Suarez, Grotius, Pufendorf, and Finnis—a roster in large measure determined by reference to Finnis' work and an understanding of the natural law tradition. Insofar as she wants to grasp the manner in which and the reasons why subsequent accounts depart from Aquinas' conceptual framework, Westerman offers a theoretical rather than an historical explanation of each theory. For a theoretical explanation prescinds from any attempt to explain the basic conceptual framework and subsequent efforts to modify it in

of Human Life (Huntington, IN: Our Sunday Visitor, 2000), 63.

terms of historically contingent circumstances and factors; precisely by bracketing such data, Westerman focuses on the various elements constitutive of each thinker's theory and seeks to determine whether these several elements can be harmonized or if tensions inevitably arise (*DNLT*, 10). Such an approach is adopted in order to show that subsequent statements of natural law, although themselves deficient, are proposed solutions to problems discerned in earlier accounts. This is important, for "[i]f it can be argued that the reformulations of the natural lawyers can be regarded as 'forced moves', in the sense that they are the only acceptable solutions to certain problems which arose on the basis of Aquinas's legacy, this would be a serious challenge to Finnis's theory, which is entirely based on that legacy" (*DNLT*, 5).

While I have been speaking of a tradition of natural law inquiry, Westerman holds that the theories under investigation do not constitute a tradition of inquiry, yet for heuristic purposes views them *as if* they constituted such a tradition (*DNLT*, 11); to this end, she advances a working-definition of natural law, an "idealized notion" which captures what is crucial to any theory of natural law, in terms of four assumptions:

> (a) there are universally and eternally valid criteria and principles on the basis of which positive law [and judgments of conscience] can be justified and/or criticized; (b) these criteria and principles are grounded in nature . . . specifically, human nature; (c) human beings can discover those principles by the use of reason; (d) for positive law to be morally obligatory, it should be justified in terms of these principles and criteria (*DNLT*, 12).[4]

These assumptions are posited for the purpose of analyzing and evaluating the theories under consideration, even if they do not say all that can be or needs to be said about natural law, and are

---

[4] The appropriateness of these criteria has been challenged by Mark C. Murphy, on the grounds that such a conception of natural law "presupposes an impossibly high standard for what it is to provide a critical measure for positive law;" see his review of Westerman in *Ethics* 109 (1999): 709-710 at 709.

augmented in the accounts of the various thinkers Westerman investigates. Westerman's major finding is that the natural lawyers themselves are not strongly committed to these assumptions, something that becomes clear when one attends to the division between "fundamentals" and "applications" in their work; though one finds a careful and detailed discussion of the manner in which the various foundational elements of natural law are interrelated and combined, one does not find, according to Westerman, a corresponding attempt to show how natural law is utilized or applied in practice. Westerman claims that natural law thinkers, including Aquinas, do not, in keeping with their professed natural law program, actually apply the theory; instead, they end up appealing to a different program, though this is not easily recognized since they continue to use the traditional categories associated with natural law (*DNLT*, 16). In finding that the foundational principles are not brought to bear upon practice, Westerman concludes that "these foundations seem to fail just because they are foundations" (*DNLT*, 17); the foundational aspirations of natural theory evidently undermine its capacity to be of practical use, and something else must be called upon to do what natural law cannot do.[5] For Aquinas, Westerman thinks that the virtue of prudence plays this supplementary role, and does so without reference to natural law; Aquinas, on this telling, is a virtue-ethicist who also happens to have a theory of natural law.[6]

---

[5] Westerman's philosophical commitments emerge here quite distinctly, as she is endorsing a version of moral particularism or ethical anti-theory. For an overview of the former, see the short essay by Michael Slote, "Moral Particularism," in the *Routledge Encyclopedia of Philosophy*, ed. Edward Craig (London and New York: Routledge, 1998) 6: 528-529; several statements of the latter are in the anthology *Anti-Theory in Ethics and Moral Conservatism*, ed. Stanley G. Clarke and Evan Simpson (Albany: State University of New York, 1989).

[6] For a short account of virtue ethics, see Daniel Statman, "Introduction to *Virtue Ethics*," in Virtue Ethics, ed. Daniel Statman (Edinburgh: Edinburgh University Press, 1997), 1-41. Recent authors who find virtue playing a foundational role in Aquinas' thought include: Daniel Mark Nelson, *The Priority of Prudence: Virtue and Natural Law in Thomas Aquinas and the Implications for Modern Ethics* (University Park, PA: Pennsylvania University Press, 1992); Pamela M. Hall, *Narrative and the Natural Law: An Interpretation of Thomistic Ethics* (Notre Dame: University of Notre Dame Press, 1994); and Jean Porter,

To offer an account of the conceptual framework of Aquinas' natural law theory is, Westerman is aware, to enter a field of interpretive controversy. Legal positivists (and others) contend that Aquinas' moral philosophy falls victim to the naturalistic fallacy, and relies on the questionable assumptions of God's existence and of a teleological view of nature (*DNLT*, 21). The question as to whether Aquinas is guilty of the naturalistic fallacy centers on the manner in which the first principles of natural law are founded. On the legal positivist reading, Aquinas advocates taking stock of one's inclinations as a way of specifying the good that is to be done and pursued, and this is considered a straightforward passage from *is* to *ought* or an attempt to derive norms from nature, as one *ought* to pursue that to which one *is* naturally inclined (*DNLT*, 24). Westerman counters this suggestion by pointing out that the normative force of the principles involving specification of the good is given by or borrowed from the first principle of practical reason—"good is to be done and pursued and evil is to be avoided";[7] as such, this radically first principle should be understood as the foundation of morality, from which additional moral rules, specifications of this first principle, are derived by appeal to our natural inclinations. On the other hand, Finnis and Germain Grisez hold that Aquinas' conception of practical reasoning does not involve any illicit move from facts to values, nor does it presuppose any assumptions about God or nature (*DNLT*, 22). Westerman interprets Finnis as positing the first principle of practical reason as a formal principle directive of all reasoning in the practical sphere; as a "methodological guideline," rather than a "normative injunction," it is necessary but not sufficient for right practical reasoning (*DNLT*, 25). Moreover, Finnis' insistence that no speculative appeal be made to nature or our natural inclinations leaves him ascribing to Aquinas, so Westerman thinks, a view of

The Recovery of Virtue (Louisville, Kentucky: Westminster/John Knox Press, 1990).

[7] *Summa Theologiae*, First Part of the Second Part, Question 94, Article 2. I have throughout this paper used the translation of this work by the Fathers of the English Dominican Province (Notre Dame, IN: Christian Classics, 1981). Further references to this work will be given in the text in the conventional manner (e.g., ST 1-2.94.2).

practical reasoning in which one "is to some extent free to deliberate on [one's] *particular conception* of the good" (*DNLT*, 26).

The obvious way to resolve this interpretive controversy and the question of whether Aquinas commits the naturalistic fallacy would be to examine the key text at the heart of the dispute—*ST* 1-2.94.2. Westerman adopts a different strategy, however, pushing the inquiry back to a consideration of the relationship between natural law and eternal law, which Aquinas holds is "the exemplar of divine wisdom as directing the motions and acts of everything" (*ST* 1-2. 93.1). She then appeals to the discipline of art to unpack what Aquinas means by exemplar, suggesting that it refers to "the idea of a work of art as a harmonious and proportionate whole, which is suitable to the end it is meant to serve" (*DNLT*, 28). God, in creating the world, and the artist, in producing a work of art, both have a comprehensive conception of their work as a harmonious whole ordered to a specified end. The exemplar within the divine mind "directs the way the world is and should be" (*DNLT*, 29), and, in view of this directive role is said to constitute a law. The eternal law is thus to be understood as a principle that regulates creation and directs it to its end, "rather than [as] a set of coercive precepts" (*DNLT*, 29). Borrowing a term from aesthetics, Westerman suggests that we may speak of the exemplar by which God orders the world as "God's style" (*DNLT*, 29). Such a term, she maintains, more adequately captures the sense of what eternal law is than does the term "law" itself, as it recognizes God as Artificer and avoids the problem of whether the eternal law imposes any obligation on God; for God freely chooses a particular style, and remains sovereign even after its adoption (*DNLT*, 30). While Westerman offers a number of additional reasons why it is fitting to understand eternal law in terms of "style," one especially important consideration is that it explains why Aquinas offers no account of our obligation to observe the requirements of natural law (*DNLT*, 33). For Westerman, the question of obligation arises only when natural law is understood as a set of precepts, and she insists that "natural law is not a set of moral rules, precepts and prohibitions" (*DNLT*, 33). Natural law is, rather, our capacity to adopt the divine style, and this style is the only style that we can possibly adopt. A discussion of one's obligation to adopt the only style that is available is unnecessary and beside the point, for "we have no other alternative than to adopt His style" (*DNLT*, 33)—though one can fail to adopt the divine style successfully.

This conception of law as style is used by Westerman to resolve the controversy surrounding the first principle of natural law. While the first principle is indeed formal, as Finnis and Grisez hold, it also serves as a general evaluative criterion as well, and so is not purely formal; it is formal in the sense that it is a general stylistic requirement, yet it is moral in the sense that by appeal to it one can determine that acts involving pursuing evil can never be evaluated as morally permissible—something that Finnis and Grisez's interpretation of the first principle of practical reason apparently fails to capture (*DNLT*, 34). This solution, however, gives rise to a further debate concerning the role played by nature or our natural inclinations in specifying the first principle. Westerman points out that the first principle is not sufficient to inform rational beings as to how to adopt the divine style; in order to determine how to adopt God's style, one must investigate God's products, the expressions of God's style, and thus the inclinations and ends in (human) nature (*DNLT*, 35). She concludes that while the legal positivist interpretation of Aquinas recognizes a role for nature, it errs because it conceives of the inference involving our natural inclinations as one that follows in an automatic or mechanical manner; as for Finnis and Grisez, Westerman thinks that they correctly identify the fallacious reasoning in the legal positivist interpretation, but erroneously claim that practical reasoning should not and need not be informed by an understanding of nature, deeming nature "entirely irrelevant for practical reasoning" (*DNLT*, 35).

Insofar as the inference from our natural inclinations to moral norms is not an automatic one, there is evidently a need to evaluate the information given by nature, and to this end Westerman claims that Aquinas appeals to two metaphysical assumptions. The first assumption is a general claim about what "the good" is or how it is to be understood; it is an assumption that Westerman thinks needs to be situated within a hierarchical and teleological framework (*DNLT*, 37), as Aquinas holds that, in general terms, "good" is to be understood as a quality of being and that all beings are to strive toward a fullness of being. As such, the first principle of natural law enjoins one to utilize one's practical reason so as to achieve the end of perfection or fullness of being to which one is naturally inclined. But to do this one needs to have recourse to the second metaphysical assumption, which refers to the inclinations that are implanted in all creatures. As these are hierarchically ordered, Aquinas is able to distinguish between ends desired for their own sake and ends desired for the sake of some further goals, between a most complete end and less complete or "sub-ends." In view of this distinction, those ends associated with the inclinations we share with substances and sentient beings are to be subordinated to those proper to rational beings alone (*DNLT*, 38-39); more specifically, there is only one complete end—the knowledge of God—and all other ends, to the extent that they possess value and are neither wholly instrumental nor complete, are to be considered "sub-ends" (*DNLT*, 40). Our practical reasoning goes right, we correctly adopt God's style, only when more complete ends are given priority to less complete ends (knowledge of God over self-preservation). On this view, Finnis' claim that Aquinas is not committed to a hierarchical conception of the human good is gravely mistaken.

Westerman realizes that her account of Aquinas, for all its talk of "style," might seem indistinguishable from the neo-Thomist view, derided by legal positivists, in which the moral injunction of the first principle of practical reason is specified by appeal to natural inclinations. The key difference, she suggests, can be seen in the manner in which a presumed textual and conceptual difficulty for Aquinas is handled in their respective accounts. For Westerman reads Aquinas as proposing two definitions of "the good," one in which it is understood as the desirable and one in which it is equated with the desired (*DNLT*, 41). This identification, or equivocation, is of no concern to neo-Thomists, as they take it as evidence that Aquinas does not make the illicit inference from is to ought, from desired to desirable. Westerman, however, thinks Aquinas' equating of the desired and the desirable leaves him with a serious difficulty of having to provide a criterion by which we can judge that certain ends are more "complete" or more "perfective" and others less so (*DNLT*, 43). If this criterion is not simply a function of the desires people actually have, then an objective criterion is required in order to determine whether one should desire what one in fact desires. But this requirement cannot be met, as Westerman maintains that, for Aquinas, "[n]o objective criterion seems to be available" (*DNLT*, 43-44). Instead, she finds Aquinas positing a different criterion in asserting that those with well-tempered affections seek the most complete conception of the ultimate end (*ST* 1-2.1.7). Westerman concludes that in order to identify the particular ends that should be desired and sought, Aquinas would simply have us look to the example of the virtuous person (*DNLT*, 44). For the virtuous person pursues ends that are disclosed by practical reason, and such reasoning "should be informed by the expression of God's style that can be found in both human nature and in the natural inclinations we share with irrational beings" (*DNLT*, 46). The information attained in this way is not to be used automatically or mechanically (as the legal positivists maintain), nor is it to be ignored (as with Finnis). Endeavoring to act in view of what is most perfective of one's nature from among the goods here and now available to one is to appropriate the divine style and to succeed as an artist of one's own.

In proceeding to examine Aquinas' attempt to bring his doctrine of natural law to bear upon individual choices and actions and the formation of laws, Westerman wants to show that his account of practical reasoning involves more than what the legal positivist recognizes and, as such, should not be written off as fallacious. As we have seen, the ends constitutive of the divine style are more or less complete, and the only criterion that enables one to determine which ends are truly desirable is the example of the virtuous person (*DNLT*, 44). This role now, inexplicably in view of the foregoing, seems to be assigned to *synderesis*,[8] for *synderesis*, according to Westerman, is the human capacity to understand the divine style immediately—that is, without any discursive reasoning (*DNLT*, 50). While the understanding of the first principle provided by *synderesis* facilitates the discovery and evaluation of further truths (*DNLT*, 52-53), these further principles are the starting points for all practical reasoning, and thus provide criteria and standards for self-constituting choices and actions. Hence, *synderesis* achieves insight into the divine style, first, by appeal to the general principle that all things should seek a fullness of being, and then with reference to the natural inclinations shared with other creatures and proper to humans (*DNLT*, 54). But, as noted above, Westerman thinks that Aquinas recognizes ends that are ordered to and thus subordinate to the ultimate end, and regards them as choice-worthy in part because they make possible the attainment of the ultimate end; as such, any end other than the ultimate end may be considered a subordinate end, and thus an object for deliberation and choice (*DNLT*, 55), so that in practice one need not be committed to pursuing or even endorsing all the ends that *synderesis* grasps. Westerman concludes that *synderesis* plays a limited role in our practical reasoning: it merely allows us to perceive that we have a general tendency, shared with all creatures, toward our own perfection and that there are several hierarchically ordered ends to which we are naturally inclined (*DNLT*, 56).[9]

---

[8] Aquinas uses this term to refer to one's acquired or habitual understanding of the first principles of natural law. See *ST* 1-2.94.1.

[9] It is worth pointing out that Westerman allows that the general tendency towards our perfection or ultimate end is captured in a moral principle that is inferred as the legal positivist suggests, that is, from the fact that all things *do* strive for their perfection and that there *is* an ultimate end for humankind; but she denies that Aquinas thinks that all moral norms are inferred in this way, for the values associated with the sub-ends need not impose any obligation upon us, as they can be overwritten by more complete ends (*DNLT*, 56).

Synderesis' grasp of the divine style must accordingly be supplemented by the insights of conscience, whose role is to apply the divine style to particular actions (*DNLT*, 57). In doing so, conscience translates the general directiveness of synderesis into more determinate norms with the aim of guiding one's choices and actions (*DNLT*, 57). It is by means of judgments of conscience, then, that one makes determinations about particular actions (*DNLT*, 57). Yet while conscience indicates what should be done or avoided in particular cases, and enables us to judge retrospectively the moral value of acts already performed, Westerman emphasizes that it is inescapably fallible. One may err in various ways in the reasoning and judgment of conscience, and these errors may require one to reformulate the specific rules or the particular conclusions that were erroneously derived from them. According to Westerman, Aquinas is of the mind that we should not have an "exaggerated confidence" in the deliverances of reason in the practical realm, for human affairs are variable and contingent and our judgments concerning them easily mistaken; we should therefore always be prepared to revise the specific rules and conclusions erroneously generated by conscience (*DNLT*, 60).

Westerman develops this last point considerably as she turns to consider the necessity of cultivating and acquiring the virtue of prudence. It is not just that, due to the variability and contingency of human affairs, we are prone to error in our moral reasoning; Westerman suggests that Aquinas holds that human nature itself is (accidentally) variable, from which she thinks it follows that we are simply unable to attain complete certainty regarding particular conclusions about human acts (*DNLT*, 61). In view of this uncertainty and of the variable and contingent features that constitute the matrix for one's choices and actions, practical reasoning cannot be understood to be a function solely of demonstrations, though we do make use of this form of inference. As we have seen, Westerman thinks that Aquinas holds up the reasoning embodied in the virtuous person as a guide for identifying the human good in its completeness and complexity, and characterizes it as "an indemonstrable wisdom" (*DNLT*, 64). So, despite the fact that Aquinas describes the role of prudence as one of ordering human actions by reasoning from general principles to specific conclusions, and that this description sounds much like the one given of conscience, Westerman notes that there is a difference between the roles assigned to each, as prudence involves both right reasoning and acting upon what reason has settled (*DNLT*, 62). Most importantly, Aquinas' account of prudence is given in terms of a descriptive list of features, of the elements essential for its acquisition and exercise, and not in terms of prescriptions, guidelines, or recipes to be followed (*DNLT*, 64). The subject matter upon which prudence sets to work renders "unequivocal answers" unobtainable, and, proceeding by way of induction, the prudent person is only able to determine what the best course of action is in most cases (*DNLT*, 64). In view of these considerations, Westerman likens the virtue of prudence to that of a skilled artist, for it similarly requires that one come to possess a special quality if one is to adopt successfully the divine style. Aquinas' refusal to give an account of prudence in terms of precepts and demonstrative reasoning is, Westerman thinks, evidence of an "awareness that humans are imperfect and that they therefore should be allowed a certain space for free deliberation about what should be done in contingent circumstances" (*DNLT*, 65).

In the area of legislation, Westerman finds a similarly negligible role for natural law and an important one for prudence. For legislators are charged with doing for the state what individuals must do for themselves, as it falls to them to derive specific rules or laws from the general principles of natural law so as to help secure the common good of their particular society (*DNLT*, 65). In performing this task, the legislator essentially recapitulates the pattern of reasoning that individuals perform in their own deliberations, though Aquinas does not employ the same set of terms in describing it. Instead, he refers to the two kinds of reasoning of the legislator as deduction and *determinatio*.[10] Deduction proceeds syllogistically, by first de-

---

[10] As Robert P. George notes, "no single word in English captures the meaning of

riving secondary precepts from the general principles that capture propositionally the basic ends constitutive of the human good, and then by further specifying these secondary precepts so as to form human law for enactment. Once again, Westerman emphasizes that there is a wide scope for error in this kind of syllogistic reasoning, in particular in the second syllogism insofar as it lacks the certain starting point of the first. As for *determinatio*, its deliverances are not arrived at deductively, but through making specific determinations from general forms or requirements, as the architect must settle on the design of a building from among a range of satisfactory alternatives. Since no one single solution to such a problem can be reached through deduction, one makes a determination appropriate to contingent circumstances and situations; as the basic principles of natural law are of little help in such determinations, the legislator, no less than the deliberating individual, must exercise prudence in dealing with such uncertainties.

Westerman argues that an understanding of the roles and uses of deduction and *determinatio* not only allows one to appreciate why the legislator requires prudence, it enables one to grasp with precision how human laws attain their moral and legal force—and this is an important consideration for any natural law theory. First, Westerman notes that the obligatory force of human laws arrived at by deduction from more basic principles of natural law is a function of natural law itself, whereas those laws that are the product of *determinatio* are, as a result of their enactment, legally but not morally binding (*DNLT*, 69). Second, and relatedly, the laws that are formed by means of deduction from natural law are thought to enjoin or prohibit things intrinsically good or evil, whereas the things that are enjoined or prohibited by *determinatio* are understood to be good or evil only through being enjoined or prohibited. Third, Westerman

---

determinatio. 'Determination' captures some of the flavor of it; but so do 'implementation,' 'specification,' and 'concretization.'" See his "Natural Law and Positive Law," in *In Defense of Natural Law* (Oxford: Oxford University Press, 1999), 108. I have accordingly let the Latin expression stand.

suggests that Aquinas does not hold that all valid human laws must be underpinned by natural law's moral force, insofar as he maintains that those laws that have their force from their enactment remain legally valid even when morally corrupt (*DNLT*, 70).

It follows that natural law is of only limited significance in the moral and legal realm: while we can be certain about the main principles grasped by *synderesis*, these cannot prevent us from falling into error in deriving laws or secondary precepts and in their application to actions; we may, moreover, lack other qualities—the elements of prudence—that are necessary in order to deploy correctly God's style. Returning, then, to the four assumptions about natural law theory with which she began, Westerman finds that they must be qualified to fit with Aquinas' account. Westerman grants that Aquinas' natural law theory accepts assumptions (b) and (c), since he allows that reason discovers general principles, founded upon human nature, which function as a criteria for human acts and laws; she points out, however, that reason can only attain certain insight into a few essential principles, and that when reasoning from these starting points errors may arise, which frustrate one's efforts to appropriate God's style (*DNLT*, 72). Westerman also recognizes that, in line with assumption (a), Aquinas thinks that these general principles can be used to justify and criticize positive law; but she points out that the criteria Aquinas identifies are of such generality that they do not make possible a detailed evaluation of legal systems. Finally, in the case of assumption (d), Westerman notes that while some human laws are morally binding, insofar as they are deduced from the principles of natural law, those based on *determinatio* are considered legally binding only and are without any moral force whatsoever (*DNLT*, 73).

Westerman concludes that, as natural law cannot deal adequately, directly, and by itself with contingent, particular human actions or with the formation of human laws, Aquinas was compelled to appeal to prudence and to attempt to find a place for it within his natural law theory (*DNLT*, 293). But Westerman argues that prudence is not an integral part of Aquinas' natural law program, and, indeed, is separable from it. Westerman's claim is that Aquinas is not alone in this failure, and she argues that successive natural law thinkers each tried—and failed—to perform the two-fold task of solidifying the foundations of natural law while also bringing it to bear upon particular conclusions in the moral and legal realms. By failing to do anything with natural law theory, and effectively, if tacitly, deploying a different program in practice, all such accounts testify to natural law's disintegration. The way forward for moral and legal philosophy, then, is to abandon the work at the level of foundations so as to concentrate on the tools and concepts that are actually employed in making concrete determinations (*DNLT*, 293).

II. AN ASSESSMENT OF WESTERMAN'S PROJECT AND A VINDICATION OF AQUINAS

In view of her understanding of natural law as the human capacity to participate in God's style, Westerman finds that Aquinas' doctrine of natural law is of limited practical significance and that it cannot preserve one from error. But her reading of Aquinas fails to incorporate some essential features of his account, and is inaccurate in places. In what follows, I merely draw attention to some of Westerman's errors, inconsistencies, and oversights, and make no effort to offer a comprehensive statement of Aquinas' moral and legal philosophy. My aim is the limited one of defending Aquinas from Westerman's objections so as to show that his account of natural law can indeed serve as a point of departure for reflection on and the development of natural law theory.

First, there is a need to question Westerman's general approach to Aquinas' doctrine of natural law. Her suggestion was that we can resolve the dispute between legal positivists and Grisez and Finnis as to whether Aquinas commits the naturalistic fallacy through an investigation of the eternal law, or God's style; in particular, her claim is that "Aquinas had created the whole edifice on the assumption that God created the world according to an ordering principle, a style, which He expressed in nature" (*DNLT*, 287). But not only is there no question of an assumption here,[11] such an approach will invite resistance from the legal positivist camp, for whom the appeal to God will be as problematic as any logical fallacy.[12] Aside from inviting unnecessary conflict, there is a good deal of textual support in Aquinas that suggests that one need not first posit that God exists in order to grasp the first principles of natural law. Westerman herself certainly has not made the case that God's existence and the additional metaphysical assumptions she appeals to must first be affirmed if natural law is to be known.

Aquinas articulates four important theses that suggest an alternative approach to the study of natural law than the one Westerman adopts. First, while the first principles of natural law are considered by Aquinas to be self-evident and indemonstrable (*ST* 1-2.91.3, 94.2), the knowledge of God's existence is not self-evident (*ST* 1.2.1) and precisely for this reason needs to be demonstrated. Accordingly, on Aquinas' view, one does not require a knowledge of God's existence, activity, or "style" in order to be able to grasp natural law's first principles; were Aquinas to hold that God's existence must be affirmed prior to one's grasping any practical principles or moral precepts, moral knowledge and culpability would be radically limited, given his view that truths about God discoverable by reason are "known by a few, and that after a long time and with the admixture of many errors" (*ST* 1.1.1). A further problem with Westerman's appeal to metaphysical knowledge for an understanding of the first principles of natural law is that it is opposed by what Finnis calls a fundamental axiom of both Aristotle and Aquinas, viz. "that one comes to understand the nature of an active reality (for example, human persons) by understanding its capacities and inclinations, and one comes to

---

[11] Aquinas maintains that the world's dependence on God as creator is a matter of philosophical demonstration. See *ST* 1.44.1.

[12] Westerman herself draws our attention to this difficulty (*DNLT*, 21), but does not see its implications for her approach to Aquinas.

understand *them* by understanding the corresponding activities, and one understands these activities by understanding their objects."[13] In the case of human activity, the objects in question are the intelligible goods that find expression in and are articulated by the first, self-evident, principles of natural law; so, whereas Westerman holds that a metaphysical understanding of (human) nature underpins our grasp of natural law, Aquinas is evidently committed to precisely the opposite position. It is our practical understanding of the objects or ends of human acts which facilitates our understanding of these acts, the powers or capacities by which we perform them, and, in turn, human nature. Since Finnis is merely following Aquinas' text on this precise point, Westerman's charge that nature plays no role at all in Finnis' account (*DNLT*, 35)—and that, as such, his approach is a Neo-Kantian one (*DNLT*, 16, 288) which leaves one free to deliberate on a particular conception of the good (*DNLT*, 26)—is inexplicable and groundless.[14] Moreover, were one with Westerman to make metaphysical knowledge a condition for grasping the first principles of natural law, this would make these principles a product of derivation and demonstration, where instead Aquinas insists that these first principles are self-evident, or indemonstrable, and therefore underived.[15] It should also be noted, finally, that Aquinas is of the view that one can come to possess moral virtue without possessing all of the intellectual virtues (cf. *ST* 1-2.58.4); among the virtues Aquinas deems unnecessary for acquiring moral virtue—wisdom,

---

[13] John Finnis, "Introduction," xvii. Finnis draws attention to this axiom and to the works of Aquinas in which it is found (e.g., in Aquinas' *Commentary on Aristotle's De Anima*, Bk. II, lect. 6, n. 308 and *ST* 1.87.3) in several of his studies. Nonetheless, he notes that "[t]his fundamental element in Aquinas' strategy as a theorist is not so much rejected as completely overlooked in much modern work on Aquinas;" see Finnis, *Aquinas*, 53.

[14] In *Natural Law and Natural Rights*, for example, Finnis affirms that "Aquinas would agree that 'were man's nature different, so would be his duties' (footnote omitted). The basic forms of good grasped by practical understanding are what is good for human beings with the nature they have" (Oxford: Clarendon Press, 1996), 34. He holds that natural law ethics is unlike Kantian varieties precisely insofar as it recognizes basic goods, and appeals, at least implicitly, to human flourishing and nature; see "Introduction," xi.

[15] See *ST* 1-2.91.3, 94.2, 100.3.

science, and art—two play a central part in Westerman's reading of Aquinas (wisdom and art). Insofar as Aquinas does not consider the virtues associated with metaphysical or speculative knowledge to be required for the possession of moral virtue, it follows that they are unnecessary for coming to understand the basic principles of natural law. Hence, the general approach to natural law through the conception of "style" confronts some serious textual obstacles.

Westerman's particular conception of the divine style is also seriously misleading insofar as it is proposed as a reading of Aquinas. There is no reason, in principle, to object to Westerman's choice to discuss natural law in terms of God's "style," for, however one refers to Aquinas' doctrine of natural law, one must do so in such a way that captures all that Aquinas thinks is included in it. But this is precisely how Westerman's account fails. First, one can observe a certain tension, if not outright incoherence, in Westerman's discussion of natural law precepts and whether the divine style is (in part, at least) constituted by them. On the one hand, there is complete denial: "[n]atural law is not a set of moral rules, precepts, and prohibitions" (*DNLT*, 33); on the other hand, Westerman acknowledges the central and irreplaceable role of the very rules that she earlier sought to excise from Aquinas' account when she explains that conscience is the act whereby "general rules are translated or processed into more specific rules and eventually into conclusions, which refer to particular cases or circumstances" (*DNLT*, 57). Westerman's denial of the truth that God's style is comprised of moral rules or precepts is thus repudiated by her own reading of Aquinas, and one must regard simply as a false opposition her insistence that "[t]he question is not to what extent we are obliged to follow precepts, but to what extent we are obliged to adopt God's style" (*DNLT*, 33). Her alternative suggestion regarding natural law—that it refers to the human capacity to appropriate the divine style (*DNLT*, 33, 46)—is straightforwardly at odds with Aquinas' text, for Aquinas is clear that natural law refers to what is *grasped* by our capacity to reason (*ST* 1-2.94.1).

Natural law, or our participation in God's style, then, is understood in terms of principles and precepts. Since this is so, it is important to identify the range, number, and kinds of precepts that Aquinas recognizes. But, here again, Westerman's study is seriously deficient, this time through the very incompleteness of her account. Like other studies of Aquinas' doctrine of natural law, Westerman's completely overlooks a host of principles and precepts whose role is crucial to living an upright life.[16] I refer here, in particular, to the positive and negative precepts that Aquinas regards as derived or secondary precepts of natural law.[17] It is true that Aquinas' discussion of these precepts occurs within the context of his treatment of the Old Law,[18] for the simple reason that a number of these precepts are found in the Decalogue; but what needs to be emphasized is that Aquinas thinks that everyone is bound to observe the precepts of the Decalogue, *precisely because they are part of the natural law* (*ST* 1-2.98.5). Also overlooked in Westerman's account is the principle from which these precepts are said to be derived. Aquinas' position is that the precepts of the Decalogue concerning one's duties to others are derived, specifically, from the self-evident principle enjoining love of neighbor (*ST* 1-2.100.3 ad 1). This leaves Thomist commentators with the problem of relating the self-evident principle that the good is to be pursued and done (and the other principles "based" on this) with the self-evident principle involving love of neighbor—a problem not even recognized, let alone addressed, by Westerman. It was Alan Donagan's considered judgment that Germain Grisez's solution to this difficulty is the only one that is consistent with Aquinas' text,[19] and I know of no reason to depart from this judgment.

---

[16] See, for a recent example, Anthony J. Lisska, *Aquinas' Theory of Natural Law: An Analytical Reconstruction* (Oxford: Clarendon Press, 1996). The error here is to treat exclusively or predominantly *ST* 1-2 qq. 90-97, when, in fact, Aquinas' treatise on law includes qq. 98-105 as well—questions that have a significant bearing on his account of natural law.

[17] Aquinas discusses and distinguishes positive and negative precepts in a number of places; see *ST* 2-2.3.2, 33.2, 79.3 ad 3, 142.2 ad 2; and *ST* 1-2.71.5 ad 3, 88.1 ad 2, 100.10 ad 2.

[18] That is, that part of divinely revealed law that is given in the Old Testament.

[19] See Alan Donagan, *The Theory of Morality* (Chicago: University of Chicago Press,

On this view, some of the first principles of natural law prescribe the pursuit of certain fundamental goods and the avoidance of what is opposed to them, while other principles and precepts concern the manner or way in which we pursue these goods and instruct us as to how we should pursue them.[20]

Aquinas explains that the negative exceptionless precepts of the Decalogue that bear upon one's duty to others apply always and everywhere and in every situation (*semper et ad semper*); this means that these negative secondary precepts of natural law—of God's style—altogether exclude from our consideration certain actions as fitting means by which to attain given ends. Since it can never be correct to choose and perform the acts proscribed by such negative precepts, they are exceptionless. As for affirmative secondary precepts, Aquinas holds that while they are true and can rightly be followed in most cases, there are occasions—deemed by Aquinas to be rare (cf. *ST* 1-2.94.5)—when a concrete consideration will create a situation in which a normally binding precept does not bind. Such positive precepts increasingly admit of exceptions as they are spelt out in greater detail, for to the increase in detail corresponds additional ways in which the precept can fail. The point that must be underscored, however, is that Aquinas recognizes that we are able to grasp affirmative secondary precepts, which may not be applicable in every situation and which may admit of exceptions, and negative precepts which guide our choices and actions by excluding certain specifiable acts as altogether unreasonable. In failing to integrate these additional precepts into her interpretation of Aquinas, Westerman is forced to provide an account of how practical determinations are made that relies on a supposed hierarchy among the fundamental ends of human action, and to claim that only the prudent, by appeal to metaphysical assumptions about human nature, attain the requisite insight into the hierarchy of ends. Even if she were correct about

---

1977), 61.

[20] This point is lucidly explained by William E. May, *An Introduction to Moral Theology*, 2nd ed. (Huntington, IN: Our Sunday Visitor, 2003), 77.

the question of whether these ends are hierarchically ordered, given that Aquinas holds that we make correct moral determinations by "judging in accordance with the whole of natural law,"[21] it is obviously critical that all relevant principles and precepts be identified so that they can be utilized for this purpose. Failing to identify such principles and precepts clearly facilitates a reading of Aquinas in which natural law is understood to be of limited practical significance, but, insofar as it is based squarely on a major oversight, such a reading is far from compelling and is easily corrected by appeal to Aquinas' text.

But there are also reasons to think that Westerman is mistaken as regards the idea that the ends of human action and living are hierarchically ordered. Her reason for positing a hierarchy among the ends identified by Aquinas is the belief that the metaphysical order in which they are presented can be translated into a scale of value (*DNLT*, 38), and the claim that Aquinas denies that the ends corresponding to the inclinations we share with all substances and other animals can be viewed as complete ends. For this controversial claim, no reference to Aquinas' text is given, nor, for that matter, does Westerman provide a reference for the claim that Aquinas' position is that knowledge of God is the "most complete end" for us (*DNLT*, 40). In assessing this position, I turn to a number of works (listed in Westerman's bibliography) which raise objections that Westerman has not considered or answered. First, Grisez and Finnis insist that order in and of itself does not imply hierarchy, and the assumption that it does is gratuitous and arbitrary; more specifically, in the case of the important question at hand (*ST* 1-2.94. 2), they ask why we should think of a metaphysical ordering of reality in terms of a hierarchical scale of value.[22] Finnis adds that this metaphysical ordering is evidently not to be interpreted as a value ranking, as it is

---

[21] See Germain Grisez, "The First Principle of Practical Reason: A Commentary on the *Summa theologiae*, 1-2, Question 94, Article 2," *Natural Law Forum* 10 (1965): 198. Grisez cites in support of this claim *ST* 1-2.91.3 ad 2, 95.2.

[22] See John Finnis and Germain Grisez, "The Basic Principles of Natural Law: A Reply to Ralph McInerny," *American Journal of Jurisprudence* 26 (1981): 29.

never used by Aquinas in any ethically relevant way, e.g., in determining which of the first principles of natural law is to be pursued, or in sanctioning harming, attacking, or setting aside a "lower" good for the sake of a "higher."[23] Robert P. George picks up this point in stating a further difficulty for the hierarchy of value thesis; George argues that, if we are given only one complete end, as Westerman suggests, this position would either require that we always choose to act in view of such an end, or otherwise fail to supply us with some intelligible grounds for determining when we should and when we should not direct our acts towards it. For these reasons, the strategy of informing and shaping our choices and actions by appeal to a hierarchy of values "seems hopeless."[24] The fundamental problem for such an approach is to provide reasons for choosing a lower-valued alternative when we know in advance that one option is simply and unqualifiedly better than any others, in the sense that it contains in itself whatever they have of value and more besides;[25] Westerman needs to explain, then, why one would ever pursue one of the less complete "sub-ends" if knowledge of God is the "most complete end" (*DNLT*, 40). It is true that one can find certain passages in Aquinas, nowhere referred to by Westerman, which seem to suggest her position regarding a privileged status among human ends for the activity of knowing and contemplating God (*ST* 1-2.3.5); but these passages do not say all that Westerman thinks they do and have to be handled with great care, as Finnis explains:

> St. Thomas, intellectualist though he may be, will point out that one can make bad use of an intellectual, but not of a moral, virtue (*ST* 1-2.57.1); indeed, he will say that, if we are considering their relationship to human activity,

---

[23] See John Finnis, *Natural Law and Natural Rights* (Oxford: Clarendon Press, 1996), pp. 94-95.

[24] Robert P. George, "Recent Criticism of Natural Law Theory," in *In Defense of Natural Law* (Oxford: Oxford University Press, 1999), 75.

[25] See Robert P. George, "Does the 'Incommensurability Thesis' Imperil Common Sense Moral Judgments?," in *In Defense of Natural Law* (Oxford: Oxford University Press, 1999), 100.

> the intellectual virtues are *less* noble than the moral (*ST* 1-2.66.3; footnote omitted). There is, we may say, no single, privileged perspective from which such a human good as theoretical knowledge grasped and enjoyed contemplatively is simply and in all respects highest, particularly if by "highest" we mean most choice-worthy.[26]

To the extent that hierarchy plays such a significant role in Westerman's interpretation of Aquinas, these considerations, which are devastating to her account, must be addressed.

In discussing how natural law can be applied to human actions, Westerman not only wants to establish that Aquinas' doctrine of natural law is of limited practical significance, but also that Aquinas allows that in our moral reasoning all sorts of errors may arise (*DNLT*, 58, 59). This allowance and admission causes her to qualify two of her guiding assumptions about natural law—(b) and (c)—, as she argues that only a few main principles can be known with certainty and that any reasoning from these involves the loss of certainty and errors (*DNLT*, 72). It must simply be said that Westerman greatly exaggerates the fallibility of practical reason in the discovery of natural law's further precepts, as a consideration of the precepts of the Decalogue reveals. For in certain passages Aquinas appears to equate the precepts of the Decalogue with the primary precepts of natural law, in that he implies that all rational agents know them immediately. Thus, for example, Aquinas writes that "the precepts of the Decalogue are such as the mind of man is ready to grasp at once" (*ST* 1-2.100 a.6). In other passages, however, Aquinas clearly distinguishes the precepts of the Decalogue and the first principles of natural law from which they are derived; but he holds that the derivation of these precepts is so simple that it is made with "very little consideration" (*ST* 1-2.100.1, 3), such that even the uneducated can readily attain this degree of moral insight (*ST* 1-2.100.11). Aquinas evidently considers the Decalogue's precepts all but self-evident,

---

[26] John Finnis, "Practical Reasoning, Human Goods and the End of Man," *Proceedings of the American Catholic Philosophical Association* 58 (1984), 27.

given the ease with which he believes they can be discovered, even if the certainty of our knowledge of them is not on par with that of the first principles. So, insofar as Aquinas maintains that everyone is obliged to observe such precepts because they belong to natural law (*ST* 1-2.98.5), we cannot follow Westerman in her claims about the fallibility of reason. For it is possible to know with certainty that certain actions are never to be done, by appeal to natural law's negative exceptionless precepts; and in the case of positive precepts, which Aquinas allows are not always applicable in a given set of circumstances, the suggestion is that they are not to be followed only in "some few cases" (*ST* 1-2.94.4) and that these are, indeed, "rare occurrences" (*ST* 1-2.94. 5).

Nonetheless, owing to the contingency of human affairs, the variability of human nature, and human imperfection, Westerman thinks Aquinas is of the view that "[c]omplete certainty cannot be reached in our conclusions concerning practical affairs" (*DNLT*, 61, 65). But Aquinas could not actually have subscribed to this position. To see this, one needs to understand Aquinas' conception of voluntariness and culpability. If, as Westerman thinks, we cannot have certainty regarding specific proposed actions, if we do not know that some actions are definitely wrong, there is no sense in which we can be culpable for them. For Aquinas holds that ignorance that is not in any way willed or the result of negligence renders an act involuntary, and thus excuses one from the evil that is (unwillingly) perpetrated (*ST* 1-2.19.6; 6.8). One is culpable only for those things that one ought to know (*ST* 1-2.19.6), and Aquinas maintains that we are all bound to know "the universal principles of right" as well as the particular duties and obligations that arise from our state in life (*ST* 1-2.76.2); in view of this kind of moral knowledge, which he maintains we all have access to, Aquinas speaks of inexcusable or vincible ignorance, which does not render an act involuntary, as it can be overcome (*ST* 1-2.19.6).

It would seem that in her attempt to assimilate morality to art Westerman failed to attend to a key difference between them which Aquinas insists upon; as the moral life involves ordering human acts in general, its central task cannot be reduced to acquiring knowledge, but also importantly includes—in a way that art does not—rectifying our appetites and passions (*ST* 1-2.57.4). Indeed, it is not the fallibility of reason that thwarts the successful application of natural law principles and precepts in the vast majority of cases, according to Aquinas, but the influence of the passions (*ST* 1-2.9.5 ad 3, 71.2 ad 3); yet even when we go astray in this way, we are still able to grasp what the right thing to do is (*ST* 2-2.155.3, 156.1), and this allows us to repent of our actions by retrospective judgments of conscience (*ST* 2-2.156.3). It is not the lack of moral insight that (typically) causes us to fall into error, according to Aquinas, but the failure to bring this insight to bear upon our choices and actions as a result of the influence of our passions and appetites. In any case, the fact that we are capable of making mistakes in our moral reasoning is not an argument against the claims of natural law theory, just as it is not an argument against the claims of mathematics.

It is also important to see that Westerman's attempt to interpret Aquinas' conception of prudence as separable from and independent of natural law fails. The first task that she assigns to prudence is that of determining the things that should be desired as goods to be pursued (*DNLT*, 43). Westerman's claim is that, as there is no objective criterion by appeal to which we can specify the degree or manner in which the various goods to which we are attracted complete or perfect us, we ought to model the example of the virtuous person (*DNLT*, 43-44); the virtuous person's behavior is to be followed because it is guided and informed by practical reason (*DNLT*, 44-45). Very well. But, again, let us investigate this position further. If there is no objective criterion by which we can judge something to be truly desirable, how does or can the virtuous person make the requisite determination? That is, the idea is that the role of the prudent or virtuous person is to determine what is truly desirable (*DNLT*, 44); but if there is no objective criterion available with which to make this determination, then how can the virtuous identify the truly desirable? Westerman suggests that the virtuous person engages in practical reasoning, and this is doubtless true; but one must ask what this reasoning is informed by, what the virtuous person reasons about. And here Westerman's story breaks apart, because she has only identified certain ends or sub-ends as following upon her metaphysical assumptions; but this kind of metaphysical knowledge is, as we have seen, not required in order to possess prudence, and, at any rate, would amount to an objective criterion. Prudence or virtue in general, then, do not stand on their own, according to Aquinas, but are informed by standards, and these standards can only be the principles and precepts of natural law, which are, in principle, knowable by all.[27]

It is therefore also necessary to reject Westerman's claims on behalf of the "indemonstrable wisdom" of the prudent (*DNLT*, 61, 64, 71), which, in practice, amounts to a kind of intuitive knowledge "that goes beyond prescriptions and guidelines" (*DNLT*, 65). Her position is that, since we cannot know with certainty whether we are choosing and acting in accord with reason, we need to follow the example of the prudent and to endeavor to acquire this virtue through actions determined in this way. Westerman thinks that the distinguishing mark of prudence is in respect to moral knowledge, as its indemonstrable wisdom alone is able to discern what is to be done in changing, contingent circumstances. Such a view, however, does not square with Westerman's own (correct) account of Aquinas' conception of conscience, as she allows that judgments of conscience do indeed reach all the way down to particular cases through the translation of general rules into specific rules and conclusions (*DNLT*, 57, 62). This view, of course, entails that through judgments of conscience those who are not-yet-virtuous can make true moral judgments, and, indeed, they must be able to do so insofar as prudence is an acquired virtue (*ST* 2-2.47.14 ad 3m, 15). Hence, as one need not possess prudence's indemonstrable wisdom in order to make concrete moral determinations, since one can appeal to spe-

---

[27] Westerman's treatment of *synderesis* seems to concede this point, even while it conflicts with her earlier account of prudence.

cific rules to do so, it remains that these determinations are made by appeal to natural law; insofar as it is by natural law reasoning that we make true moral judgments, it is natural law that accounts for the acquisition of prudence and enables us to identify who the virtuous person is. Aquinas' doctrine of natural law implies that, contrary to what Westerman suggests, one cannot otherwise appeal to the virtuous person as a standard for our moral reasoning.

As for Westerman's claim that Aquinas' account of prudence, in view of our very imperfection, acknowledges that we "should be allowed a certain space for free deliberation about what should be done in contingent circumstances" (*DNLT*, 65), a number of important clarifications are called for. First, to the extent that Aquinas accepts this claim as to what we should be allowed, his acceptance would not be given simply in view of our imperfections. Aquinas is not committed to the view that, since things are complex and complicated and we are imperfect, we should (therefore) be entitled to choose freely any option available as if there were no moral truth at stake. Here it is worth considering an important dissimilarity between good and evil acts that Aquinas recognizes: while an act deficient in any respect is considered evil, good acts must be good in every relevant respect (*ST* 1-2.18.4 ad 3). Given this conception of the morality of human acts, the first task for anyone—so Aquinas thinks—is to ensure that, by appeal to negative exceptionless precepts, no evil is done (*ST* 1-2.72.6 ad 2); only then is one to turn to pursue the good enjoined by the affirmative precepts. In this way, Aquinas recognizes "degrees of virtue" corresponding to the avoidance of evil and to the pursuit of good. The reason why Aquinas allows for free deliberation in certain contingent circumstances should now be clear: the available options among which one is free to choose will be those options that remain after one has excluded other options judged to be unacceptable by appeal to the negative exceptionless precepts.[28] As one ought not to deliberate about

---

[28] For a fuller discussion of this point and the one in the immediately following sentence, and of how they are overlooked in accounts of the moral life based on an "incommunicable

whether or how one should violate a negative precept, the sort of free deliberation Aquinas has in mind concerns acts that are at least free of obvious evil; this entails that, in a given set of circumstances, there may be more than one morally permissible thing to do—a state of affairs difficult to account for when one posits, as Westerman does, a hierarchy of value, since it presupposes that one cannot definitively determine that a given option has all the benefits promised by the others and more besides.

In view of what has been established as a corrective to Westerman's account of Aquinas' natural law theory, it is possible to deal very briefly with her reasons for thinking that natural law plays a limited role in the legal realm. Westerman concludes that Aquinas does not provide adequate criteria for the evaluation of the correctness of human laws and of legal systems, and that, as such, her first assumption about natural law (a) is in need of qualification in Aquinas' case; but it is now evident that this judgment was reached with an insufficient understanding of the range and number of natural law precepts recognized by Aquinas and of the certainty with which he thinks we can grasp them. What makes this claim all the more extraordinary is the fact that natural law thinkers in the Thomist tradition in the very period during which Westerman was writing her book (but before and after as well) used natural law reasoning to establish positions concerning the legality of such issues as abortion, euthanasia, same-sex marriage, pornography, property and welfare rights. As the positions taken on this range of concerns are established by natural law reasoning that is essentially Thomist in nature, the claim that Aquinas' account of natural law does not have the resources with which to evaluate laws or legal systems is rather implausible. As for Westerman's claim that her fourth assumption (d) needs modification insofar as the process of enacting laws by *determinatio* yields laws that are merely legally but not morally

---

wisdom"—as Westerman's is—see John Finnis, *Moral Absolutes: Tradition, Revision, and Truth* (Washington, D.C.: The Catholic University of America Press, 1991), 103-105.

binding, this also is at odds with Aquinas' text.[29] It is true that Aquinas suggests that laws that are the product of *determinatio* "have no other force than that of human law" (*ST* 1-2.95.2), and, on the strength of this isolated text, one could perhaps infer that one therefore has no strictly moral obligation to obey such laws. It should be noted, however, that Aquinas is here saying more than his own position allows;[30] indeed, earlier in the very same article he agues that "every human law has just so much of the nature of law, as it is derived from the law of nature" (*ST* 1-2.95.2). Since this is so, one should understand the moral force of a law to be derived both from its being enacted and from its intelligible relation to natural law's principles and precepts.[31] Though laws enacted by *determinatio* may be chosen from a set of equally reasonable alternatives, and thus are not strictly required by reason, once enacted and to the extent that they are found to be in accord with the principles of justice they are indeed, contrary to Westerman's claim, morally binding (*ST* 1-2.96.4)—even if defeasibly so.[32]

In summary, Aquinas' text does not support Westerman's allegation that natural law has no practical use and that prudence performs the roles that are commonly assigned to natural law. Instead, it proposes that natural law plays an important—indeed integral—role in moral and legal reasoning. Westerman does, of course, mention another reason for thinking that natural law has disintegrated, namely, that problems intrinsic to Aquinas' doctrine of natural law compelled Suarez to alter and develop it by adopting a different set

---

[29] This issue is the one occasion in which Westerman ventures to cite a text from the later questions on law in the *ST*. Unfortunately, she misreads the text at hand. Whereas she wants to show that laws enacted by *determinatio* are not morally binding, the text she refers to—*ST* 1-2.100.9—deals with another matter entirely, as Aquinas is merely explaining that we do not need to observe precepts in the manner in which the virtuous do (that is, from a virtuous disposition). This, of course, is not to say that we are not morally bound to observe the precepts—as Westerman thinks.

[30] John Finnis, *Aquinas*, 267.

[31] Ibid.

[32] Ibid., 272. Aquinas lists a number of ways in which enacted laws would not be morally binding insofar as they are judged to be unjust; see *ST* 1-2.96.4.

of assumptions regarding God's creation, law and nature (*DNLT*, 78-79). But while Westerman explains that Suarez adopted a set of alternative assumptions, she does not, in accord with her expressed objective, establish that this involved a "forced move" in view of the deficiencies of Aquinas' account. We are told *that* Suarez deviates from Aquinas, but what must be established is that he *must* do so; Westerman fails to make this case, and is forced to conclude that "it is unclear why Suarez started from a different view of creation, and why he did not endorse Aquinas' conception of eternal law" (*DNLT*, 103). Accordingly, one may interrupt Westerman's narrative at this point and return to Aquinas' doctrine of natural law as one that can be profitably developed and built upon. This is not to say that Aquinas' natural law theory is the last word on natural law, only that, by appeal to it, one can resist the charge that natural law theory has disintegrated.[33]

---

[33] I am grateful to Professor Joseph Boyle for his helpful and insightful comments on this paper.

LET'S SKILL ALL THE LAWYERS: SHAKESPEAREAN LESSONS ON THE NATURE OF LAW
Harold Anthony Lloyd

I. SHAKESPEARE AND THE LAW

Despite his limited formal education,[1] Shakespeare's works display a great deal of legal knowledge.[2] As we shall see, Shakespeare's characters and storylines present intriguing explorations of legal theory and provide good examples of how such theory can go wrong and how such theory can go right. In this article, I shall explore four of the various philosophical views (or parts of views) of the law found within his plays. Among these various views, Shakespeare explores what we would now call a form of legal positivism (i.e., the theory that laws are simply commands of the sovereign) and shows us how such an approach cannot succeed. Shakespeare also beautifully lays out arguments for natural law only to demolish them. Centuries before Holmes formulated his prediction theory, Shakespeare explores a prediction theory of the law (i.e., that the law is a set of predictions as to how the courts will act in certain circumstances) and shows us how this theory fails. Finally, Shakespeare gives us insightful bits and pieces from which we might generate a workable jurisprudence complying with the semiotics of law and its inherent restraints.[3]

---

[1] See Stanley Wells, *Shakespeare: A Life in Drama* (NY: W. W. Norton & Co. 1995), 15, who claims that Shakespeare's formal education ended by the age of fifteen.

[2] See Daniel J. Korstein, *Kill All the Lawyers? Shakespeare's Legal Appeal* (Princeton: Princeton University Press, 1994), xi-xvii (hereafter Korstein); Mark Andre Alexander, "Shakespeare's Knowledge of Law: A Journey Through the History of the Arguments," http://www.shakespearefellowship.org/virtualclassroom/Law/index.htm

[3] As Shakespeare will help us see, nothing (including law) is simply given in itself. We impose our own meanings on everything we study or do. However, as Emily Dickinson notes, community sets firm semantic limits:

> Much Madness is divinest Sense -
> To a discerning Eye -
> Much Sense - the starkest Madness -
> 'Tis the Majority

II. POSITIVISM

A. Introduction

One of the best known forms of positivism holds that laws are commands of a sovereign who is habitually obeyed and who is beholding to none other.[4] If commanded by that sovereign, laws are valid without regard to their moral content.[5] Instead, they are obeyed to avoid the predictable punishment that would ensue if they are not obeyed.[6] Shakespeare and logic both make short order of any such concept of law.

B. John, Richard II, Henry IV, Hamlet and the Problem Of Legitimate Sovereignty

Taking Shakespeare's "history plays" in their internal chronologi-

---

> In this, as all, prevails -
> Assent - and you are sane -
> Demur - you're straightway dangerous -
> And handled with a Chain –

Emily Dickinson, *The Poems of Emily Dickinson,* ed. R. W. Franklin (Cambridge: Belknap Press 1998), 278. That is not to say, however, that such meanings cannot shift or change over time. They can with proper persuasion, thus highlighting the inseparability of law and rhetoric even at law's most fundamental levels. For a nice discussion of semantic communities and their resistance to change, see Robert Benson, *The Interpretation Game* (Durham: Carolina Academic Press, 2008), 74-75 (hereafter Benson). By "semiotics of law" I therefore mean the study of legal terms, provisions and discourse within their current, generally accepted semantic framework.

[4] Edwin W. Patterson, *Men and Ideas of the Law* (NY: Foundation Press 1953), 86-87 (hereafter Patterson). Positivism takes on other forms. For example, Hart defines positivism as "...the simple contention that it is in no sense a necessary truth that laws reproduce or satisfy certain demands of morality, though they often have done so." H. L. A. Hart, *The Concept of Law* (NY: Oxford University Press, 1997 2d ed.), 185-186 (hereafter Hart). As we shall see, this form of positivism runs afoul of certain inherent restrictions of the semiotics of law which do effectively parallel certain moral restraints.

[5] Patterson *op. cit.,* 87.

[6] *Id.* at 86. If one believes in the concept of divine right of kings, the threat of punishment would also come from an awful cosmic level. See, e.g., William Shakespeare, *The Tragedy of King Richard The Second,* I,ii, 37-38, Stephen Orgel and A.R. Braunmuller, eds., (NY: Penguin Books, 2002), where Gaunt refers to Richard II as "God's substitute" and "His deputy annointed in his sight..." (hereafter *Richard II*).

cal order, *The Life and Death of King John* (hereafter *King John*) explores both the nature of sovereignty and its legitimacy. In this play, John has usurped the crown from Arthur,[7] the son of John's older brother Geoffrey. Challenging John's legitimacy, the Frenchman Chatillon therefore begins the play with a snide reference to John's "borrowed majesty."[8] To complicate matters further, John has a half-brother, Philip the Bastard, who is also the son of John's father, Richard I.[9]

Under these facts, what makes John and not Arthur or Philip the Bastard the king? Assuming for the sake of argument that the people now habitually obey John after the death of his father Henry II, where do we find John's sovereignty and legitimacy in these facts? Is it because the people fear him more? If so, what distinguishes John from a mere criminal that the populace habitually obeys out of fear of physical harm?[10] To distinguish John from such a mere criminal, the law must look beyond the common trait of force since common traits of course make no distinction. Law on its face must therefore be more than mere orders and threats. After Macbeth has lost his ethos as a leader, Angus understands this well:

> Those [Macbeth] commands move only in command,
> Nothing in love. Now does he feel his title
> Hang loose about him, like a giant's robe
> Upon a dwarfish thief.[11]

---

[7] This is not factually accurate but serves Shakespeare's purposes in the play. John's brother Richard I actually named John his heir and his succession followed after some uncertainty. See W. L. Warren, *King John,* (NY: Barnes & Noble Books, 1996), 48-50.

[8] William Shakespeare, *The Life and Death of King John*, Stephen Orgel and A.R. Braunmuller, eds.,(NY:Penguin Books, 2002), I, i, 4 (hereafter *King John*).

[9] There is no clear single historical personage corresponding to the Bastard but, again, the character serves Shakespeare's purposes in the play. All the political plays contain historical liberties and I shall correct none further. I make these initial observations simply to caution the reader to learn his or her actual political history of the times from other sources.

[10] As Hart points out, the interregnum problems under this theory run deeper still. Must not all of Henry II's laws die with him since one cannot obey the dead? Must there not always be an extended interregnum between "sovereigns" since habits require time to be acquired? *See* Hart, *op cit* 52-55.

[11] William Shakespeare, *Macbeth* V, ii, 19-22, Stephen Orgel and A.R. Braunmuller,

Any "sovereign" who claims no more legitimacy than the power to sanction if disobeyed must find the garments of state ill fitting indeed.[12] As King Lear points out, such a sovereign only holds "office" in the sense that a guard dog holds office over beggars and thieves that flee his bite. As Lear quips, "There thou might'st behold the great image of authority—a dog's obeyed in office."[13] Legal office surely means more than this. Isabella is surely correct when she claims:

> . . . it is excellent
> To have a giant's strength, but it is tyrannous
> To use it like a giant.[14]

Shakespeare also shows us that defining law in terms of threats or sanctions not only fails at the level of the "sovereign." It also fails at the level of the "subject." For if threat of sanction is required for law, then no law exists in its absence. Thus, Falstaff sees himself beyond the law when he is under no threat of punishment or sanction. He rejoices when Prince Hal is to succeed his father Henry IV because he believes that he can then "take any man's horses. . ."[15] without threat of sanction. Falstaff understands that criminal acts are decriminalized under such a theory whenever no realistic threat of sanction exists under the circumstances.[16] Such fluid criminality is hardly consistent with rule of law.

---

eds., (NY: Penguin Books 2002), (hereafter *Macbeth*).

[12] This leads us to a further difficulty with positivism. It is certainly logically possible to imagine a community with a set of laws which it simply obeys and which were never promulgated by a sovereign. When Henry V, for example, takes the throne, he requests the Lord Chief Justice to continue to assist him in application of the laws of England as he had done for his father, Henry IV. See William Shakespeare, *The Second Part of King Henry The Fourth,* V,iii, 102-145 (hereafter *2 Henry IV*). Henry V thus realizes that English law is more than edicts of sovereigns but also includes ancient rights and traditions. *Id.*

[13] William Shakespeare, *King Lear: A Conflated Text,* IV, vi, 157-159, Stephen Orgel and A.R. Braunmuller, eds., (NY: Penguin Books, 2002) (hereafter *King Lear*).

[14] William Shakespeare, *Measure for Measure,* II, ii, 107-109, Stephen Orgel and A.R. Braunmuller, eds., (NY: Penguin Books, 2002) (hereafter *Measure For Measure*).

[15] *Henry IV, op. cit.,* V, iii, 136.

[16] The sanction element creates still further problems since many legal acts involve no sanctions at all (such as procedural or donative transfer laws). See Hart, op. cit., 27-33.

However, notwithstanding these difficulties from an earthly perspective, might the command theory work if reformulated on a more heavenly level? Might the theory work if God commands, under threat of divine sanction, obedience to the earthly "sovereign"? John certainly attempts this approach. Thus, he messages that "meddling priest," the pope:

> . . . [N]o Italian priest
> Shall tithe or toll in our dominions,
> But as we (i.e., John) under God are supreme head,
> So under him that great supremacy,
> Where we do reign, we will alone uphold,
> Without th'assistance of a mortal hand.[17]

Granting *arguendo* the existence of such a God, has John not therefore potentially solved his problem? For if God commands something must it not be legitimate?

The problem here, of course, is that even if we accept some notion of the divine right of kings, we cannot as a practical matter determine who holds that right. First, the very disagreement between John and the supporters of Arthur (including the Pope himself) itself demonstrates this. Second, anyone who would appeal to God as ground for his office is not only in the awkward position of contradicting Biblical provisions on the inscrutability of divine will (such as, for example, the story of Job) but would, like Dido's sister, reject much classical wisdom on the subject as well.[18]

---

[17] *King John, op. cit.*, III, i, 153-158.

[18] Dido's sister overconfidently believes that Aeneas has come to stay and wed Dido:

> Surely by dispensation of the gods
> And backed by Juno's will, the ships from Ilium
> Held their course this way on the wind. Sister,
> What a great city you'll see rising here,
> And what a kingdom, from this royal match!

Virgil, *The Aeneid*, tr. Robert Fitzgerald (NY: Everyman's Library, 1992), 96-97 (hereafter Virgil). Aeneas was indeed driven by fate and the gods but for a very different purpose and to a very different end. Dido and Carthage were but a stop on the way to Aeneas' fated founding of the Roman race. The sister's hubris ignores the endless other possible

Not surprisingly, John himself ultimately concedes his sophistry. Finding himself in the end reduced to a wretched figure, he laments as he burns with fever:

> There is so hot a summer in my bosom
> That all my bowels crumble up to dust.
> I am a scribbled form, drawn with a pen
> Upon a parchment, and against this fire
> Do I shrink up.[19]

Richard II also relies upon divine command as his source of legitimate authority. As he puts it:

> Not all the water in the rough rude sea
> Can wash the balm off from an anointed king.
> The breath of worldly men cannot depose
> The deputy elected by the Lord. . . .[20]

With the "security" of such "anointing," Richard II recklessly banishes his cousin Henry Bolingbroke for six years and subsequently confiscates the property of Bolingbroke's father, John of

---

interpretations of these facts just as Jerry Falwell, for example, did in attributing the September 11 bombings to the wrath of God. See ACT UP, "Rev. Falwell Blames for Terrorist Attacks" http://www.actupny.org/YELL/falwell.html

[19] *King John, op. cit.,* IV, vii, 30-34. Palladas gives us further classical wisdom on this point in one of his more memorable poems:
They say Sarapis spoke within a dream

> To a killer one night sleeping underneath
> A failing wall: "Poor wretch, get up and seek
> Another place to sleep." The man complied.
> The wall collapsed right after he had moved.
> His life so spared, the villain then rejoiced
> Believing that Sarapis must approve
> Of murderers. The man gave sacrifice
> Of thanks for his escape when morning came.
> Sarapis spoke again to him at night:
> "You think I guard the evil? You escaped
> A painless death to die upon a cross."

Palladas, *The Complete Palladas* tr. Harold Anthony Lloyd (CreateSpace, 2010), 15.

[20] *The Tragedy of King Richard The Second,* III, ii, 54-57, Stephen Orgel and A.R. Braunmuller, eds., (NY: Penguin Books, 2002) (hereafter *Richard II*).

Gaunt. Bolingbroke not surprisingly rebels and raises an army to reclaim his rights. Still resting on divine rights, Richard II philosophically comforts himself:

> For every man that Bolingbroke hath pressed
> To lift shrewd steel against our golden crown,
> God for his Richard hath in heavenly pay
> A glorious angel. Then, if angels fight,
> Weak men must fall; for heaven still guards the right.[21]

When further challenged on his sovereign status as king, Richard exclaims:

> If we be not, show us the hand of God
> That hath dismissed us from our stewardship;
> For well we know no hand of blood and bone
> Can gripe the sacred handle of our scepter,
> Unless he do profane, steal, or usurp.[22]

Richard II then confidently prophesies:

> Tell Bolingbroke, for yond methinks he stands,
> That every stride he makes upon my land
> Is dangerous treason. He is come to open
> The purple testament of bleeding war.
> But ere the crown he looks for live in peace,
> Ten thousand bloody crowns of mothers' sons
> Shall ill become the flower of England's face,
> Change the complexion of her maid-pale peace
> To scarlet indignation, and bedew
> Her pastor's grass with faithful English blood.[23]

Unfortunately for Richard, his prophecy lacks present bite and Bolingbroke forces Richard to abdicate and transfer the throne to Bolingbroke (the future Henry IV).[24]

Of course, Bolingbroke (now Henry IV) can find small security in the deed. Having ousted Richard, Henry IV finds himself back in

---

[21] *Id.*, lines 58-62.
[22] *Id.*, III, iii, 91-100.
[23] *Id.*, lines 85-100.
[24] *Id.*, IV, i.

King John's same uneasy state. With John's and Richard's examples as precedent, Richard's dire prophesy must cause Henry IV much concern. If usurpers cannot maintain certain sovereignty either by appeal to God or by physically seizing the crown, tumultuous times likely lie ahead. Thus, Henry IV laments at the end of the play that he is full of woe "[t]hat blood should sprinkle me to make me grow."[25] He is right to lament. The cycles of earthly and heavenly sovereign appeal continue their predictably bloody courses through the two parts of *King Henry the Fourth*, *The Life of King Henry the Fifth*, the three parts of *King Henry the Sixth*, and *The Tragedy of King Richard the Third*.

Similar bloody cycles also play out outside the "history plays." For example, in *The Tragical History of Hamlet Prince of Denmark* (hereafter *Hamlet*), Claudius has murdered the king (Hamlet's father), married Hamlet's mother and assumed the kingship. Although we might think that God would not have endorsed such a result, how do we know this with certainty sufficient to justify the killing of Claudius? How can Hamlet know that Claudius was not in fact acting out God's will? Hamlet of course cannot know this and, confounded, he falls into a bloody, downward spiral that leaves, among others, his mother, Claudius, and himself dead.[26]

C. *Falstaff and Amorality*

In addition to the sovereign legitimacy problems generated by sovereign-command positivism, the theory generates further unacceptable substantive difficulties. If law is simply the command of the sovereign given under threat of sanction, then the content is irrelevant. Evil or nonsensical laws would be law if they are commanded by the sovereign and are obeyed out of fear of sanction.

Falstaff is of course the epitome of one who believes that the sovereign can command what he will. Thus Falstaff tells Prince Hal (the future Henry V):

[25] *Id.*, V, vi, 45-46.
[26] See William Shakespeare, *The Tragical History of Hamlet Prince of Denmark* , Stephen Orgel and A.R. Braunmuller, eds., (NY: Penguin Books 2002) (hereafter *Hamlet*).

> Marry, then, sweet wag, when thou art king, let not us that are squires of the night's body be called thieves of the day's beauty. Let us be Diana's foresters, gentlemen of the shade, minions of the moon; and let men say we be men of good government, being governed as the sea is, by our noble and chaste mistress the moon, under whose countenance we steal.[27]

For those interested in the rule of law, such implications of command-theory positivism are of course no more appealing than the other difficulties we encountered with the theory.

D. Command Theory Insight

Although Shakespeare helps us to see how the command theory fails at both the earthly and heavenly levels, he nonetheless helps us to see two insights that such theory's failure brings. First, any adequate jurisprudence must account for the symbiotic relationship between the governed and those who govern. Although the notion of the habit of obedience under threat of sanction fails to account for the law, it does reflect the fact that no legal system can work if it is not accepted by a sufficient majority of the "governed." To this point, Shakespeare has John foolishly ask, "Doth not the crown of England prove the king?"[28] No matter how securely he holds the physical crown and no matter how many times he might use it to crown himself "king," John of course has no kingly powers if a sufficient majority of the governed do not recognize him as their king. Thus, Salisbury challenges John on superfluous crownings:

> ... [T]o be possessed with double pomp,
> To guard a title that was rich before,
> To gild refined gold, to paint the lily,
> To throw a perfume on the violet,
> To smooth the ice, or add another hue
> Unto the rainbow, or with taper light

---

[27] William Shakespeare, *The First Part of King Henry The Fourth*, I, ii, 23-29, Stephen Orgel and A.R. Braunmuller, eds., (NY: Penguin Books, 2002) (hereafter *1 Henry IV*).

[28] *King John*, *op. cit.*, II, i, 273.

> To seek the beauteous eye of heaven to garnish,
> Is wasteful and ridiculous excess.[29]

Second, any jurisprudence which defines law in terms of commands, threats and sanctions may explain a dog "in office"[30] or the "authority" of any other menacing figure. It does not, however, demarcate legitimate legal authority from mere force or account for interregnal legal continuity. Rules or standards of legitimacy and continuity are required for such things. The failure of command-positivism therefore helps us to see that law must involve standards or rules.[31]

III. NATURAL LAW: ESSENCE AND INQUISITION

A. Introduction

Such failure of both earthly and heavenly command-theory positivism leads one to explore natural law as an alternative. Ulysses in *The History of Troilus and Cressida* (hereafter *Troilus and Cressida*) neatly sums up the proper social and moral order one natural law approach would seek:

> The heavens themselves, the planets, and this center
> Observe degree, priority, and place,
> Insisture, course, proportion, season, form,
> Office, and custom, in all line of order,
> And therefore is the glorious planet Sol
> In noble eminence enthroned and sphered
> Amidst the other; whose med'cinable eye
> Corrects the influences of evil planets
> And posts, like the commandment of a king,
> Sans check to good and bad. But when the planets
> In evil mixture to disorder wander,
> What plagues and what portents, what mutiny,

---

[29] *Id.*, IV, ii, 9-16.
[30] *Id.*, IV, vi, 157-159.
[31] *See* Hart, *op. cit.*, 80 (noting that ". . . the ideas of orders, obedience, habits, and threats, do not include, and cannot by their combination yield, the idea of a rule, without which we cannot hope to elucidate even the most elementary forms of law.")

> What raging of the sea, shaking of earth,
> Commotion in the winds, frights, changes, horrors,
> Divert and crack, rend and deracinate,
> The unity and married calm of states
> Quite from their fixture? [32]

B. Polixenes, Prospero and the Essence of the Natural

Despite Ulysses' beautiful words, Shakespeare makes us question not only whether any such rigid and objective natural order exists but whether it could possibly exist. In *The Merchant of Venice*, Solanio notes that "Nature hath framed strange fellows in her time."[33] As nature framed these "strange fellows," how can they not be natural? Is everything not therefore natural? Is such law based on or derived from such nature not simply therefore the law of whatever happens to be from time to time? If so, what moral or legal guidance can be found in such "natural law"?[34]

Further dismantling any such notion of "natural law," *The Winter's Tale* makes quick work of the natural order's purported immutability by simply considering plants. In the play, Perdita eschews some "unnatural" flowers that would beautify her then-barren garden:

> ... [T]he fairest flowers o' th' season
> Are our carnations and streaked gillyvors,
> Which some call nature's bastards. Of that kind
> Our rustic garden's barren, and I care not
> To get slips of them.[35]

---

[32] William Shakespeare, *The History of Troilus and Cressida*, I, iii, 85-101, see forward to 124. (Stephen Orgel and A.R. Braunmuller, eds., [NY: Penguin Books, 2002]) (hereafter *Troilus And Cressida*).

[33] William Shakespeare, *The Merchant of Venice*, I, i, 51, Stephen Orgel and A.R. Braunmuller, eds., (NY: Penguin Books, 2002) (hereafter *Merchant Of Venice*).

[34] Philosophers have struggled since at least the time of Hume to understand how an "is" could beget an "ought." See David Hume, *A Treatise of Human Nature*, P. H. Nidditch ed. (Oxford: Clarendon Press, 2d ed. 1978), 469-70.

[35] William Shakespeare, *The Winter's Tale*, IV, iv, 81-85, Stephen Orgel and A.R. Braunmuller, eds., (NY: Penguin Books, 2002) (hereafter *Winter's Tale*).

Polixenes pragmatically replies:

> ... [S]weet maid, we marry
> A gentler scion to the wildest stock,
> And make conceive a bark of baser kind
> By bud of nobler race. This is an art
> Which does mend nature--change it rather--but
> The art itself is nature.[36]

In other words, the art of botanical engineering is itself part of nature.

This bucolic exchange calls out the lie of an immutable normative natural order at its most basic level. If we truly believed in such an order, we would live naked, raked with diseases (since it would be unnatural to cure them), and we would take our barren fields simply as we found them. Of course, no reasonable person would find strict adherence to this "natural" order moral or even legal. For not only would it injure oneself should one follow it, it would injure anyone or anything entrusted to one's care.

Polixenes makes another profound though perhaps less obvious point. Such a purely "natural" life is not only undesirable, it is not possible. We must alter nature to survive. We must breathe in nature's air and thereby change it. We must eat nature's produce which we change to flesh and dung. We must rearrange its stones and grass when we walk. In short, we must alter nature to live. As life itself is surely also "natural" and more precious than grass or stones, then the art of living must be the ultimate "natural" thing. In other words, again, "[t]he art itself is nature."[37] If this is so, "natural law" takes us back to ourselves and how we would live within that world in which we are thrust. "Natural law" as something outside of and higher than ourselves therefore makes no sense for living creatures who must elevate themselves above nature.

Shakespeare takes Polixenes' point to its logical limits in *The Tempest*. In that play, Prospero's art so thoroughly determines na-

---

[36] *Id.*, lines 92-97.
[37] *Id.*, line 97.

ture that one can rarely discern what is "real" and what is not. Prospero summarizes the extent of his works when he renounces his art:

> ... I have bedimmed
> The noontide sun, called forth the mutinous winds,
> And 'twixt the green sea and the azured vault
> Set roaring war; to the dread rattling thunder
> Have I given fire and rifted Jove's stout oak
> With his own bolt; the strong-based promontory
> Have I made shake and by the spurs plucked up
> The pine and cedar; graves at my command
> Have waked their sleepers, oped, and let 'em forth
> By my so potent art .....[38]

As we must thus make ourselves by changing nature, we can hardly look to nature as an objective legal or moral guide.

C. *Grand Inquisitors*

Belief that laws are decreed by nature further begets inquisitors and tyrants like Angelo in *Measure for Measure*. When reviving unenforced morality laws, the Duke leaves Angelo in charge of the revival. By doing so, he hopes both to test the effect of revival and to reduce the potentially more severe impact that might occur if enforced directly in the Duke's name. Thus, the Duke tells the Friar:

> We have strict statutes and most biting laws,
> The needful bits and curbs to headstrong weeds,
> Which for this fourteen years we have let slip,
> Even like an o'ergrown lion in a cave,
> That goes not out to prey. Now, as fond fathers,
> Having bound up the threat'ning twigs of birch,
> Only to stick it in their children's sight
> For terror, not to use, in time the rod
> Becomes more mock'd than fear'd. So our decrees,
> Dead to infliction, to themselves are dead,
> And liberty plucks justice by the nose,

---

[38] William Shakespeare, *The Tempest,* V, i, 41-50, Stephen Orgel and A.R. Braunmuller, eds., (NY: Penguin Books, 2002) (hereafter *The Tempest*).

> The baby beats the nurse, and quite athwart
> Goes all decorum.[39]

Unfortunately for Claudio in the play, the strict language of the unenforced law provides the death penalty for him. He has committed the capital crime of impregnating a woman out of wedlock, and Angelo sees no flexibility in enforcement. Moral codes require strict enforcement to maintain justice and a commensurate high level of fear. Thus, Angelo coldly opines:

> We must not make a scarecrow of the law,
> Setting it up to fear the birds of prey,
> And let it keep one shape, till custom make it
> Their perch, and not their terror.[40]

With respect to the particular long dormant law violated by Claudio, Angelo ruthlessly states:

> The law hath not been dead, though it hath slept.
> Those many had not dared to do that evil
> If the first that did th' edict infringe
> Had answered for his deed. Now 'tis awake,
> Takes note of what is done, and like a prophet,
> Looks in a glass that shows what future evils,
> Either new, or by remissness new conceived,
> And so in progress to be hatched and born,
> Are now to have no successive degrees,
> But, ere they live, to end.[41]

When Angelo thus takes his charge, Shakespeare helps us to see how belief in fixed natural law breeds improper character traits in rulers. Since impious leaders must also mold nature to survive, their "natural" law will of course fit their evil characters. If left to their own devices, impious leaders will therefore "naturally" cultivate hubris, immorality, self-centeredness and a resulting lack of true compassion for others. Lucio summarizes this well:

---

[39] *Measure for Measure, op. cit.*, I. iii 19-31.
[40] *Id.*, II, i 1-4.
[41] *Id.*, II, ii 90-99.

> Upon [the Duke's] place,
> And with full line of his authority,
> Governs Lord Angelo, a man whose blood
> Is very snow-broth; one who never feels
> The wanton stings and motions of the sense,
> But doth rebate and blunt his natural edge
> With profits of the mind, study and fast.
> He - to give fear to use and liberty,
> Which have for long run by the hideous law,
> As mice by lions - hath picked out an act
> Under whose heavy sense [Claudio's] life
> Falls into forfeit. He arrests him on it,
> And follows close the rigor of the statute
> To make him an example.[42]

Shakespeare also shows us how natural law breeds hypocrisy. As Angelo (like everyone else) must change nature to live, his "natural" law spares him from the hated law and even allows him to demand that Claudio's sister sleep with Angelo to spare her brother.[43] Why not? If left to his own devices, the nature he molds will center around him. Fortunately, the Duke intervenes and stops Angelo. Consistent with his more virtuous nature, the Duke imposes his own more heavenly mold on nature:

> He who the sword of heaven will bear
> Should be as holy as severe;
> Pattern in himself to know,
> Grace to stand, and virtue go;
> More nor less to others paying
> Than by self-offences weighing.
> Shame to him whose cruel striking
> Kills for faults of his own liking.
> Twice treble shame on Angelo,
> To weed my vice and let his grow.
> O, what may man within him hide,
> Though angel on the outward side!
> How may likeness, made in crimes,

---
[42] *Id.,* I, iv, 55-68.
[43] *Id.,* II, iv, 140-169.

> Making practice on the times,
> To draw with idle spider's strings
> Most ponderous and substantial things?[44]

Although the Duke's words are impressive, they bring little comfort from a "natural" law perspective. The next Duke might have the character of an Angelo.

D. Among the Clouds

The problems with any such natural law run deeper still. Even if the objectively natural exists, we can find no fixed or objective measure of it. Not only do Angelo and the Duke disagree on eternal matters of morality, Hamlet reminds us how even mere clouds are subject to multiple interpretations. Thus, Hamlet muses with Polonius:

> HAMLET Do you see yonder cloud that's almost in shape of a camel?
> POLONIUS By th' mass and 'tis, like a camel indeed.
> HAMLET Methinks it is like a weasel.
> POLONIUS It is backed like a weasel.
> HAMLET Or like a whale.
> POLONIUS Very like a whale.[45]

Further, as Theseus notes in *A Midsummer Night's Dream,* diverse dispositions dictate different interpretations of nature. Taking three types of persons, he remarks:

> The lunatic, the lover, and the poet
> Are of imagination all compact.
> One sees more devils than vast hell can hold:
> That is the madman. The lover, all as frantic,
> Sees Helen's beauty in a brow of Egypt.
> The poet's eye, in fine frenzy rolling,
> Doth glance from heaven to earth, from earth to heaven,
> And as imagination bodies forth
> The forms of things unknown, the poet's pen

---

[44] *Id.*, III, ii, 249-264.
[45] *Hamlet, op. cit.*, III, ii, 369-375.

> Turns them to shapes, and gives to airy nothing
> A local habitation and a name.[46]

Theseus also notes how easily persons of any disposition often confuse themselves: "[I]n the night, imagining some fear,/ How easy is a bush supposed a bear!"[47]

If nature is so elusive even with its mere vapors and bushes, *a fortiori* must not graver notions of "natural" morality elude our sight and expression? In fact, what we can see of nature suggests *no* normative standards beyond those we would impose. Shakespeare frames his great *As You Like It* upon this very point. In that play, the characters may either live in court (where others' rules are imposed upon them and upon "nature") or in the wild (where each individual may attempt to impose his or her own rules including even gender rules).

When Duke Senior escapes to the woods of Arden, he is therefore free to say, "Here we feel not the penalty of Adam. . ."[48] Comparing the woods to court, he can also fancifully ask, "Hath not old custom made this life more sweet/ Than that of painted pomp?"[49] He can therefore attempt to impose his more pleasing paradigm of "old custom" upon the wild where one may live free of any taint of original sin.[50] Yet, Duke Senior recognizes and is "irked" by the butchery of nature required to live "naturally":

> Come, shall we go and kill us venison?
> And yet it irks me the poor dappled fools,
> Being native burghers of this desert city,
> Should in their own confines, with forkèd heads
> Have their round haunches gored.[51]

---

[46] William Shakespeare, *A Midsummer Night's Dream*, V, i, 7-17, Stephen Orgel and A.R. Braunmuller, eds., (NY: Penguin Books, 2002) (hereafter *Midsummer Night's Dream*)

[47] *Id.*, 21-22.

[48] William Shakespeare, *As You Like It*, II, i, 5, Stephen Orgel and A.R. Braunmuller, eds., NY: Penguin Books 2002) (hereafter *As You Like It*).

[49] *Id.*, 2-3.

[50] *Id.*, 2-5.

[51] *Id.*, 21-25.

Jacques (a person the First Lord labels a "melancholy" man[52]) is also troubled by such killing. With such a disposition, Jacques naturally has a much darker view of Arden. The First Lord describes having seen him earlier in the day:

> Today my Lord of Amiens and myself
> Did steal behind him as he lay along
> Under an oak …
> To the which place a poor sequestered stag,
> That from the hunter's aim had ta'en a hurt
> Did come to languish…and thus the hairy fool,
> Much markèd of the melancholy Jacques,
> Stood on th' extremest verge of the swift brook,
> Augmenting it with tears.[53]

From Jacques' perspective, Arden is hardly paradise. Instead, it is colored by his own unique melancholy free of others' paradigms. As he puts it himself:

> I have neither the scholar's melancholy, which is emulation; nor the musician's, which is fantastical; nor the courtier's, which is proud; nor the soldier's, which is ambitious; nor the lawyer's, which is politic; nor the lady's, which is nice; nor the lover's, which is all these: but it is a melancholy of mine own, compounded of many simples, extracted from many objects, and indeed the sundry contemplation of my travels, which, by often rumination, wraps me m a most humorous sadness.[54]

Though Jacques and the Senior Duke live in the same state of nature, they clearly live in different worlds.

These same "natural" worlds not only differ spatially but temporally as well. As Rosalind observes in the play, "Time travels in divers paces with divers persons."[55] Time trots for

> … a young maid between the contract of her marriage

---

[52] *Id.*, 26.
[53] *Id.*, 29-43.
[54] *Id.*, IV, i, 10-19.
[55] *Id.*, III, ii, 301-302.

> and the day it is solemnized. If the interim be but a sennight, Time's pace is so hard that it seems the length of seven year.[56]

Yet, time "ambles" for those who sleep easily or have merry lives, "gallops" for the thief on the way to the gallows and stands still for lawyers sleeping between their terms.[57] Nature thus allows for endless variation (conceptual, spatial and temporal) with no obvious normative guidance. How could it possibly give us objective laws?

This problem of course not only plagues natural law theory based upon "objective" nature as found in Arden or elsewhere. It also plagues at least three other forms of "natural law" theory which purport to rest upon objective criteria beyond the flux of mutable human categories and perspectives.[58] One such alternative theory of "natural law" rests upon the view of men and women as teleological creatures who should learn and seek their proper ends. Under this view, true laws could be defined as those which advance such proper ends while "law" which runs counter to such proper ends would not be truly law.[59] Although notions of ultimate ends and goods and of aspirations thereto may be useful instruments of ethical discourse, the claims that men and women truly have objectively-discernable "goods" or "ends" to which they should strive must of course suffer from the very same problems that plague such objective claims

---

[56] *Id.*, 306-309.

[57] *Id.*, 310-324.

[58] These three additional forms of natural law do not exhaust the number of additional possible "natural law" theories but I believe they are further exemplars of problems inherent in any theory of law based upon the objectively given or the objectively "natural." For a more exhaustive discussion of different forms of "natural law" theory see Patterson, *op. cit.*, 332-375 and J. M. Kelly, *A Short History of Western Legal Theory*, 19-21, 57-63, 102-104, 141-146, 186-189, 222-229, 258-271, 333-334, 374-380, 418-430 (Oxford: Clarendon Press, 1994) (hereafter Kelly).

[59] For example, Aristotle states, "Every art and every inquiry, and similarly every action and choice, is thought to aim at some good; and for this reason the good has rightly been declared to be that at which all things aim." Aristotle, *Nicomachean Ethics* 1094a1-3, W. D. Ross, tr., *The Complete Works of Aristotle* (Princeton: Princeton University Press, 1991). A detailed examination of Aristotle's legal and political theory is beyond the scope of this article.

about nature itself. Any "natural law" derived from such teleological notions must therefore prove as subjective and fallible as any "natural law" based upon or derived from nature itself.

Another approach to "natural law" defines such law in terms of reason. One formulation by Cicero provides a good example:

> True law is right reason in agreement with nature; it is of universal application, unchanging and everlasting; it summons to duty by its commands, and averts from wrongdoing by its prohibitions."[60]

Yet, to be comprehended, reason, too, must of course be framed and categorized no less than Hamlet's clouds. Reason therefore cannot be objectively "in agreement with" nature.

A third approach to "natural law" would invoke the law of God.[61] However, this approach must also of course suffer from the same difficulties plaguing the two prior forms just discussed. For man to understand and apply such law of God, such law must be communicated and must serve as the object of human thought. But this of course again injects the same relativity we have just seen. "God's law" will depend upon the categories and temperaments of the persons who study and expound it. It cannot reveal itself or be revealed in any purely objective fashion that is not ultimately centered in the realm of variable human thought. In fact, such natural law theorists find themselves vexed with the very problems that plague command-theory positivists who invoke the notion of the divine right of kings. For, again, even if we accept some notion of the divine right of kings, we cannot as a practical matter determine who holds those rights. The many bloody sovereignty disputes throughout history leave little doubt on this point. And, again, anyone who would appeal to God to ground his office not only awkwardly con-

---

[60] Patterson, *op. cit.*, 342-343. Cicero's meaning of "nature" is not always clear in his various passages. See *id.* However, this passage suggests law as reason in the sense I wish to note.

[61] Gratian for example related " natural law to the Decalogue and to Christ's commandment of love of one's neighbour. . . ." Kelly, *op. cit.*, 142.

tradicts Biblical provisions on the inscrutability of divine will (such as, again, the story of Job) but fails to learn from ancient wisdom on such folly.[62]

All this is not to say, however, that law cannot have essential (and in that sense perhaps "natural") restraints upon it *within* cognitive or semiotic systems. As we shall see in Section V below, at least ten such restraints exist where law is understood as a system of rules effectively governing social behavior.

IV. PREDICTION THEORY

A. Introduction

If command-theory positivism and the natural law theories just examined do not work, one might be tempted simply to define law in terms of experience with the courts and other officials. Holmes took this view when he maintained that the law is simply a set of predictions of what the courts will do in given circumstances.[63] Thus, if I say that murder is illegal, I am saying that I believe some court will likely punish me if I commit the act. If I advise that a certain clause in a contract is valid and binding, I am simply predicting that courts will enforce it.[64]

B. Falstaff and Laws as Predictions

Falstaff certainly believes that the law is little more than the workings of a judicial system which can be predicted and manipulated. Thus, viewing the law as a forecast of the latitude he believes he will receive once Prince Hal accedes to the throne as Henry V, Falstaff exults:

> [T]the laws of England are at my commandment. Blessed

---

[62] Again, they would make the mistake of Dido's sister who overconfidently believes that Aeneas has come to stay and wed Dido when instead Dido and Carthage are but a stop on the way to Aeneas' fated founding of the Roman race. Virgil, *op. cit.,* 96-97.

[63] Patterson, *op. cit.,* 119-120.

[64] See *Id.*

are they that have been my friends, and woe to my lord chief justice!⁶⁵

Although Prince Hal may have also shared a similar view while still a prince, such a view will of course not work once Hal becomes king. As king, the law is something he must apply and it does not make sense to say that he is merely predicting what he will do when he applies the law. When he was on the other side of the law, Henry might have amused himself with the fancy that law is simply a prediction of what actions enforcement officials might take. But as king, his official actions are actions, not predictions of actions. As a logical matter, he can no longer play Falstaff's game. He therefore rejects Falstaff⁶⁶ and asks the Chief Justice to assist him instead in the application of English law.⁶⁷

V. SEMIOTIC THEORY

A. Introduction

As Shakespeare has shown us, stable legal systems cannot rest upon questionable foundations (such as sovereign commands under threat of sanction, natural law in the forms explored above or law as mere prediction.) As he also helped us see with the failure of command-theory positivism, any such stable systems must involve standards or rules.⁶⁸ For purposes of the remainder of this article, I shall therefore work from what I believe to be several uncontroversial, high-level statements about the nature and purpose of law. First, the general purpose of the law is to provide "guides to human conduct and standards of criticism for such conduct."⁶⁹ These guides are normally provided for the "primary purpose of setting the citizen's relations with other citizens. . ."⁷⁰ This guidance is accomplished by

---

⁶⁵ *Henry* IV, V, iii, 137-139.
⁶⁶ *Id.*, V, v, 47, 56-59
⁶⁷ *Id.*, V, iii 102-145.
⁶⁸ See again Section III(D) of this article.
⁶⁹ Hart, *op.cit.*, 249.
⁷⁰ Lon Fuller, *The Morality of Law* (New Haven: Yale University Press, rev. ed., 1969),

"subjecting human conduct to the governance of rules."[71] One could refine this understanding of law further[72] but this start should suffice for purposes of this article. If we take this general approach, Shakespeare helps us recognize the following things about "law" as so understood. First, law requires some degree of compliance by those putatively subject to it. As *Richard II* shows us, it does not suffice for Richard II to believe that he is king; his "subjects" must act in such a way as well. Thus, there must be some workable mechanism for determining whether a system of laws is in place and, if so, who its officials are. Second, assuming such a legal system exists, one must of course have some workable mechanism for validating law within it. Without such a mechanism, we are left with no way, for example, to settle the potential desuetude of the old statutes Angelo would enforce in *Measure for Measure*. Third, as Angelo also demonstrates, there must be some workable mechanism for changing such statutes should they remain in full force and effect. Fourth, as Angelo's recalcitrance in his conviction and sentencing of Claudio also shows, law must be subject to reasonable adjudication. Fifth, as Angelo further shows, confusing law with morality actually creates moral difficulties. Since morality is generally considered fixed at any given time[73] the old statutes could not be altered in time to spare Claudio if they are confused with morality.[74] This would, of course, violate the third principle stated above. Sixth, to restrain the Angelos in office, we must understand what law *qua* law permits and prohibits (which I shall call law's inherent restraints). We shall explore each of these six areas in turn.

207-208 (hereafter *Morality Of Law*).

[71] *Id.* at 46.

[72] For example, Hart notes that law is distinguished from other bodies of rules by, *inter alia*, its "general claim to priority over other standards." Hart, *op. cit.*, 249.

[73] See *id.* at 175-178. This is not to say that moral notions cannot evolve and improve over time and that people cannot make deliberate attempts to foster such evolution. However, morality by its nature changes gradually where it changes at all. Law, on the other hand, must have flexibility to adapt immediately as the circumstances require.

[74] *See* Hart, *op. cit.*, 175-178. I shall discuss the risks of such mixture in further detail in Section VI(5) of this article.

B. Six General Requirements

1. Compliance Requirement

For any legal system to exist, a substantial majority must accept its rules. By this, I mean that a substantial majority must accept such rules as a behavioral guide. For example, "A accepts the rule that he should drive on the right side of the road" means that A drives on the right side of the road *because* the rule tells him to do so. It does not mean that he drives on the right side simply out of habit or because all other people seem to do so or because he thinks it is the safer side to drive on the right side. "Acceptance" in this sense occurs as and when rules apply to a situation at hand. Such acceptance is testable by watching A's behavior *and* by asking him why he is behaving in such a way.[75] (Of course, this standard of general acceptance must be a relative one which admits more flexibility as the importance of specific laws decrease. For example, we should most certainly say a legal system fails if half of the population disobeys its highest court half of the time. Yet we would not necessarily say that a legal system fails because half of the population jaywalks half of the time.)

Again, *Richard II* gives us a powerful example of the perils of ignoring such facts on the ground. Believing that he is divinely ordained and therefore divinely protected, Richard infers that he need not consider his subjects' behavior. Thus, Richard overconfidently claims when discussing Bolingbroke, the future Henry IV:

> Not all the water in the rough rude sea
> Can wash the balm off from an anointed king.
> The breath of worldly men cannot depose
> The deputy elected by the Lord.
> For every man that Bolingbroke hath pressed
> To lift shrewd steel against our golden crown,
> God for his Richard hath in heavenly pay

---

[75] Acceptance is thus not a concept of continuous conscious acceptance which would potentially make the law go in and out of existence as people slumber, examine their need for allegiance or think on other things.

> A glorious angel. Then, if angels fight,
> Weak men must fall; for heaven still guards the right.[76]

Of course, Richard II soon learns that legal systems do not depend upon angels, waterproof balms or physical crowns. They instead require testable compliance. Had he performed such tests and acted accordingly, he might have kept his life, his physical crown and whatever kingly power he possessed.

2. Grounding Requirements

Actual compliance with a legal system of course requires a means of determining both the content of the system as well as the legitimate officials of the system. One cannot comply with unknown rules or officials and one does not comply when one follows false rules or officials. In *Richard III*, Shakespeare gives us a chilling yet verbally clever account of the chaos that ensues when sovereignty and law are shifting and unclear. Queen Elizabeth (wife of Edward IV), Queen Margaret (Widow of Henry VI) and the Duchess of York (the mother of Richard III, Edward IV and Clarence) are together on stage while the latter two lament the deaths caused by Richard III's meddling with the grounds of royal succession:

> QUEEN MARGARET :. . . Tell over your woes again by viewing mine.
> I had an Edward [Edward, Prince of Wales], till a Richard [Richard III] killed him,
> I had a husband [Henry VI], till a Richard [Richard III] killed him:
>
> *(To Queen Elizabeth)*
>
> Thou hadst an Edward [Prince Edward], till a Richard [Richard III] killed him;
> Thou hadst a Richard [Richard, Duke Of York], till a Richard [Richard III] killed him.

---

[76] *Richard II, op. cit.*, III, ii, 54-62.

> DUCHESS OF YORK: I had a Richard [Richard III's father] too, and thou didst kill him;
> I had a Rutland [her youngest son] too, thou holp'st to kill him.
>
> QUEEN MARGARET: Thou hadst a Clarence too, and Richard [Richard III] killed him.
> From forth the kennel of thy womb hath crept
> A hellhound that doth hunt us all to death . . . . [77]

Before his death by Richard III's sword, Henry VI had foretold such chaos:

> And thus I prophesy: that many a thousand
> Which now mistrust no parcel of my fear,
> And many an old man's sigh, and many a widow's,
> And many an orphan's water-standing eye—
> Men for their sons', wives for their husbands',
> And orphans for their parents' timeless death—
> Shall rue the hour that ever thou wast born.[78]

Of course, Henry VI also reaped the fruit of similar contempt for the foundation of legal order. Henry VI "inherited" his throne from Henry V, heir of Henry IV. As noted earlier, Henry IV "acquired" his throne through the forced abdication and murder of Richard II. Before Henry IV seized the crown, the Bishop of Carlisle gave his own chilling prophecy:

> The blood of English shall manure the ground,
> And future ages groan for this foul act;
> Peace shall go sleep with Turks and infidels,
> And in this seat of peace tumultuous wars
> Shall kin with kin and kind with kind confound;
> Disorder, horror, fear and mutiny
> Shall here inhabit, and this land be called
> The field of Golgotha and dead men's skulls.

---

[77] William Shakespeare, *The Tragedy of King Richard The Third*, IV, iv 39-48, Stephen Orgel and A.R. Braunmuller, eds., (NY: Penguin Books, 2002) (hereafter *Richard III*).

[78] William Shakespeare,*The Third Part of Henry The Sixth*, V, vi, 39-43, Stephen Orgel and A.R. Braunmuller, eds., (NY: Penguin Books, 2002) (hereafter *3 Henry VI*).

> O, if you raise this house against this house,
> It will the woefullest division prove
> That ever fell upon this cursèd earth.
> Prevent it, resist it, let it not be so,
> Lest child, child's children, cry against you woe![79]

With his powerful metaphor of the house divided against itself, the Bishop underscores the lesson of *Richard III* that legal systems collapse without a stable ground, i.e., without generally accepted rules determining current law and officials.[80]

These plays therefore highlight four important points about such basic legal grounds. First, as Richard II learns through his ouster, the question of their existence turns on whether a sufficient majority accept the grounds as validating rules for the system.[81] As Richard II also learns though his ouster, such acceptance is measured as and when the issue comes into play. Of course, in the case of

---

[79] *Richard II op. cit.,* IV, i, 142-149.

[80] Richard III and Henry IV might defend their actions in terms of the arbitrariness of the fundamental grounds of any legal system. To avoid infinite regress, fundamental grounds of legal systems (like basic grounds of any other systems) can require no grounds themselves. Richard III and Henry IV might therefore respond that nothing of moral significance has occurred as a result of their usurpations since they have merely substituted one arbitrary ground for another. However, in addition to being self-defeating (since the same argument could equally be turned on them), the argument would miss the point of such basic grounds. Their sole purpose is to support a broader structure which collapses when they are removed. Just because one's neighbor arbitrarily chose bricks instead of stone as the foundation for his house, it does not follow that one may rightfully demolish the house by removing its "arbitrary" foundation. It also misses the point that systems resting upon such "arbitrary" grounds may be evaluated by multiple criteria including morality and effectiveness of purpose. Bloody and chaotic systems violating such evaluation risk rejection by those whose acceptance is required for such systems' very existence.

[81] On the point of grounds and validity, Hart correctly notes, "We only need the word 'validity', and commonly only use it, to answer questions which arise *within* a system of rules...." *See* Hart, *op. cit.,* 108-109. We do not, therefore, apply the term to the ultimate standards or grounds of a system itself but to the rules within the system. Those tests themselves are simply accepted as proper measures just as the standard meter bar in Paris is posited as the standard metric measure. *Id.* (Hart takes this example from Wittgenstein who notes, "There is *one* thing of which one can say neither that it is one metre long, nor that it is not one metre long, and that is the standard metre in Paris." Ludwig Wittgenstein, *Philosophical Investigations,* G.E.M. Anscombe, tr., (Oxford: Blackwell 3d ed., 2001), §50 at 21e.

many legal rules, the issue potentially only arises at the official level since the public may, for example, never concern themselves with the more technical rules of law.[82] Second, as all the history plays show, ground or basic rules can be criticized as immoral. They can be criticized as counterproductive. They can be criticized for any reason whatsoever which is external to the system of rules.[83] If such criticism holds and sways sufficient opinion, it can destroy such ground or basic rules by eliminating the recognition required for them to hold. Third, nothing logically forbids ground rules from incorporating moral elements. Richard II and King John, for example, do this when they assert their divine right to rule. However, so doing involves the risks of confusing law and morality discussed in this article,[84] risks one need not take to have a moral legal system.[85] Fourth, Hamlet's cloud problem discussed in Section IV(D) above of course also apply here. Ground rules are also seen through the eyes of the beholder and are therefore subject to interpretive dispute. Where such dispute exists, resolution comes either through force or verbal persuasion. Rhetoric therefore plays a critical role at the most fundamental levels of the law and is therefore inseparable from any full analysis of the law.

3. Means of Change

As the world and as community standards change, the law must of course keep pace or become at best irrelevant, at worst misguided or even detrimental to the state and thus the legal system itself. As Coriolanus puts it in *The Tragedy of Coriolanus* (hereafter *Coriolanus*):

---

[82] See Hart, *op. cit.*, 116-117.
[83] See note 78 *supra*.
[84] See note 71 *supra* and related text and Section VI(F) of this article.
[85] One may construct a legal system compatible with a given morality without incorporating that morality in the legal system's ground rules. For example, if a given morality requires equal protection and due process for all, one may ground a legal system with a constitution that requires equal protection for all and provides due process for all. The moral system itself need not be incorporated to achieve that result.

> What custom wills, in all things should we do't [i.e., if we do it],
> The dust on antique time would lie unswept
> And mountainous error be too highly heaped
> For truth t' o'er-peer....[86]

One can see no clearer example of "unswept" statutes than those statutes Angelo would enforce against Claudio (but not himself) in *Measure for Measure*. The need to correct these laws goes beyond the issue of fairness to Claudio. In truth, the need for change goes to the very survival of the state and thus the law itself. To this point, Pompey asks the ancient Lord Escalus in the play, "Does your worship mean to geld and spay all the youth of the city?"[87] Taking the statutes literally might well require action to such effect (if not worse) and that would of course ultimately destroy the city. Pompey therefore prophesies that if the law is enforced for ten more years, he "... will rent the fairest house in [the city] after threepence a bay ...."[88] He knows that rental prices will collapse because demand will disappear as people do.

As laws interact with the governed in a legislative or deliberative manner, constitutional, statutory and regulatory change must be possible and accomplished as required. As laws also interact with the governed in a forensic or judicial manner, change must also be possible and accomplished here. A state which does not permit appropriate legislative or judicial[89] change not only risks unfairness but eventual annihilation. Should Angelo have his way in both such areas, he might well prove the last man standing (no pun intended), a feat of course due only to his hypocrisy.

---

[86] William Shakespeare, *The Tragedy of Coriolanus,* II, iii, 117-120, Stephen Orgel and A.R. Braunmuller, eds., (NY: Penguin Books, 2002) (hereafter *Coriolanus*).

[87] *Measure For Measure*, *op. cit.*, II, i, 232-43.

[88] *Id.,* 255-56.

[89] In addition to their interpretive naïvetés demonstrated by Hamlet's cloud problem, those who claim instead that judges should "simply enforce the law as it is" make their beds with Angelo and share his misplaced arrogance, hypocrisy and recklessness with respect to the future of the state.

4. Means of Adjudication

Shakespeare helps us see that even long-held and "settled" law cannot be applied unthinkingly. Application involves judgment and flexibility as required by the facts (which themselves, like Hamlet's cloud, are of course always subject to interpretation). In *Measure for Measure*, Claudio cannot be automatically condemned even if one accepts the old statutes as valid. First, Claudio has a potential defense.[90] Second, it would warp even the old statutes if he were improperly convicted because it would change their meaning by having them do what they were not intended to do. Thus, even Angelo "dressed in a little brief authority" must give Claudio a fair, reasonable and objective hearing or risk violating the laws himself.[91]

5. The risks of confusing law with morality

Hart gives several cogent reasons for maintaining a clear distinction between law and morality. First, as we have seen, mixing law and morality makes the law too difficult to change since morality is generally considered fixed at any given point in time.[92] We cannot simply decree that good is now evil or evil is now good—if morality evolves such evolution requires a gradual and often highly-contentious process. We can of course reword statutes but their moral import must remain the same if law and morality overlap.

---

[90] Claudio claims he has a "true contract." *Measure for Measure, op. cit* I,ii, 144-154.

[91] Even if Claudio does not succeed with his legal defense, the law must also provide for the possibility of mercy or reprieve. This follows as a straightforward logical matter since one cannot anticipate (as Claudio's predicament illustrates) all the possible consequences of any law. If a possible consequence of a law is inconsistent with the purpose of a law, application of the law in that case of course makes no sense (and may in some cases even effectively violate the law if the result is what the law meant to proscribe). The law must allow, indeed, that in at least some situations:

> The quality of mercy is not strained;
> It droppeth as the gentle rain from heaven
> Upon the place beneath. It is twice blest:
> It blesseth him that gives and him that takes.

Merchant of Venice, IV, i, 182-185.

[92] See Section V(A) and Hart, *op. cit.*, 175-178.

This does not, however, make the law truly flexible or subject to real change. Claudio would find no solace in a reworded statute that still demands his death.[93]

Hart also wisely notes that confounding law and morality gives bad laws an aura of morality that makes them difficult to challenge even if such laws are otherwise easily changeable.[94] Consistent with Hart's concerns, Angelo clearly demonstrates the potential immorality such confusion can cause in the name of morality. Whether Angelo is a true zealot or a hypocrite using "morality" for his own ends, natural law theory as he wields it creates horrendous problems for both the individual and the state. As we have seen above, Angelo's enforcement of the old statutes not only wrongly threatens Claudio with death but it threatens the very survival of the state itself.[95]

Furthermore, as Hart notes, confusing law and morality generates the analytical problems that flow from adulteration of any concepts. Just as we would confound economic analysis by confusing "money" with "gold" or confuse physics by confounding "atoms" with "points," we would confuse legal analysis by mixing law and morality. As Hart puts it:

> A concept of law which allows the invalidity of law to be distinguished from its immorality, enables us to see the complexity and variety of these separate issues; whereas a narrow concept of law which denies legal validity to iniquitous rules may blind us to them.[96]

If we wish to understand the concept of law, we are therefore

---

[93] One might argue that laws can change under a natural law approach because we may be confused in what we consider good or evil. Once we see our error, we can and should change the law accordingly and law therefore can and should change. However, in addition to ignoring the problem of Hamlet's cloud, changing the law in such a case concedes the point that law and morality were not the same before the change and thus need not be the same.

[94] *See* Hart, *op. cit.*, 210-212.

[95] *See* Sections III(C) and V(B)(3) above.

[96] Hart, *op. cit.*, 211.

more likely to succeed if we analyze the concept shorn of all extraneous notions. Claudio's predicament demonstrates this well. Angelo reads his rigid view of morality into the statutes. However, the Duke also reads a very different and more lenient morality into them.[97] Whose reading is correct? We have Hamlet's cloud problem here not only at the inevitable level of the words of the statutes themselves but also at the further level of the conflicting moral elements they putatively contain. What is to be gained by this double complexity? Reasoned legal discourse will surely more likely succeed if we can first agree on the meaning of the rule itself and then turn to the moral implications of that meaning as a separate question. One Hamlet cloud problem at a time (rather than two intermingled cloud problems compounding questions upon themselves) surely increases the odds of successful, reasoned discourse.

Finally, these points lead to Hart's observation that a wider concept of law permits a broader study of rules including what makes rules "iniquitous."[98] The merits of this, I believe, speak for themselves.

6. The Semiotic Decalogue
i. Law and the Requirement of Rules

Again, for purposes of this article, I accept what I believe to be those several uncontroversial statements about the purpose and nature of law previously set forth. Summarizing them again, the general purpose of the law is to provide "guides to human conduct and standards of criticism for such conduct."[99] These guides are normally provided for the "primary purpose of setting the citizen's relations with other citizens. . . ."[100] This guidance is accomplished by "subjecting human conduct to the governance of rules."[101] Again,

---

[97] *See Measure for Measure, op. cit.*, III, ii, 249-264.
[98] See Hart, *op. cit.*, 207-212.
[99] See note 66 *supra*.
[100] See note 67 *supra*.
[101] See note 68 *supra*.

we could refine this understanding of law further[102] but this start should suffice for purposes of this article. If we take this general approach, Shakespeare helps us to see at least ten inherent requirements that apply to any legal system regardless of its political stripe or persuasion.[103]

First, there must of course be rules. In *The Second Part of Henry The Sixth*, the rebel Cade well understands that a lawless society cannot have rules. Thus, he would create an incoherent England under his command:

> There shall be in England seven halfpenny loaves sold for a penny, the three-hooped pot shall have ten hoops, and I will make it felony to drink small beer . . . .[104]

Consistent with the legal vacuum such abolition of rules must entail, Butcher announces his famous line: "The first thing we'll do is kill all the lawyers."[105] Cade goes beyond this; he orders the demolition of the Inns of Court and the burning of all the records of the realm.[106] Surely if Cade and his followers succeed in such endeavors, there can be no law in England. Abolishing all rules in any other realm would of course have the same effect.

ii. The Requirement of Public Rules

Since unknown rules cannot be intentionally followed, it of course follows that rules must be public if they are to be standards of conduct for a person or persons.[107] Although no further proof

---

[102] See note 69 *supra*.

[103] The first seven requirements listed below generally conform with Fuller's requirements. See *Morality of Law, op. cit.,* 39. See also Hart, *op. cit.,* 207.

[104] William Shakespeare, *The Second Part of Henry the Sixth,* IV, ii 70-72, Stephen Orgel and A.R. Braunmuller, eds., (NY: Penguin Books, 2002) (hereafter *2 Henry VI*).

[105] *Id.*, line 81. As we learn shortly later, their target includes more than lawyers. They also mean to kill "[a]ll scholars, lawyers, courtiers, [and] gentlemen . . . ." *Id.,*IV, iv 35-36.

[106] *Id.*, IV, vii. 1-2, 13.

[107] Hart makes an important distinction between viewing rules from an internal or external point of view. Rules are viewed from an internal perspective if they are accepted as guides for conduct. They are viewed from an external perspective if they are simply predictions as to how people will behave. See Hart, *supra* note 4, at 89. Since a secret

seems required, Shakespeare gives us an amusing example of this requirement. In *The Taming of the Shrew*, Petruchio first redefines rules of language without publicly so stating:

> PETRUCHIO Come on, a God's name; once more toward
>   our father's.
> Good Lord, how bright and goodly shines the moon!
>
> KATE The moon? the sun. It is not moonlight now.
>
> PETRUCHIO I say it is the moon that shines so bright.
>
> KATE I know it is the sun that shines so bright.[108]

Should Kate continue to use the standard rules of English grammar, the two will be in a confounded stalemate. Petruchio of course knows this and therefore makes his new rules clear:

> PETRUCHIO Now, by my mother's son, and that's myself,
> It shall be moon or star or what I list,
> Or e'er I journey to your father's house.[109]

With his rule now public (that rule being: things are called whatever I call them from time to time), Kate can play along and things move forward without further difficulty. Thus, she "concedes":

> KATE Forward, I pray, since we have come so far,
> And be it moon or sun or what you please.
> An if you please to call it a rush candle,
> Henceforth I vow it shall be so for me.
>
> PETRUCHIO I say it is the moon.
>
> KATE   I know it is the moon.

---

rule is unknown, it of course cannot be accepted as a standard of conduct. However, an outsider who does not know the rule might be able to infer its existence externally, i.e., as an external rule of behavior of those in-the-know persons who embrace it internally.

[108] William Shakespeare, *The Taming Of The Shrew* V, v, 1-5, Stephen Orgel and A.R. Braunmuller, eds., (NY: Penguin Books, 2002) hereafter *Taming Of The Shrew*.

[109] *Id.*, lines 6-8.

> PETRUCHIO Nay, then you lie. It is the blessèd sun.
>
> KATE Then, God be blessed, it is the blessèd sun,
> But sun it is not, when you say it is not,
> And the moon changes even as your mind.
> What you will have it named, even that it is,
> And so it shall be still for Katharine.[110]

iii. *The Requirement of Understandable Rules*

For the same reasons that rules must be public to be accepted as rules of conduct, they must of course also be understandable. Petruchio and Kate's dialogue above can also be seen as illustrative of this point. Calling the sun "the moon" would not be comprehensible to the average person and could hardly serve as a workable guide for conduct without further explanation. For example, if Petruchio asks a third party to paint a picture of the "moon" without further explanation, that third party will of course paint a picture of the moon and not the sun as Petruchio means.

iv. *The Requirement of Possible Performance*

If law is to govern behavior, it of course cannot do so if it requires the impossible. For persons cannot comply with the impossible and that by definition defeats the very purpose of a rule.[111] One could give comical examples of this absurdity such as requiring men every fifth of March to dance on the head of a pin. Shakespeare, however, shows us in *Lucrece* that the matter is far from humorous. In this poem, Lucrece "follows" a "rule" which she of course cannot follow: she must under no circumstances have sex with a man other

---

[110] *Id.*, lines 12-22.

[111] One might object that impossible rules can serve as guidance if the purpose of the rule is to confound, i.e., to guide behavior into a confounded state. That would, however, equivocate on the term "to guide." Rules do not "guide" persons externally as strings "guide" kites across the sky. Instead, rules set standards of behavior which one either accepts or refuses to accept. Thus, a person who believes that he must square a circle on the fifth of March would in the rule-bound sense be guided to square a circle, not to confound himself.

than her husband. When she is raped, she finds herself in a logically-generated moral quandary that gives her no guidance for future behavior. Thus, she turns upon herself and her very existence:

> Out, idle words, servants to shallow fools,
> Unprofitable sounds, weak arbitrators!
> Busy yourselves in skill-contending schools;
> Debate where leisure serves with dull debaters;
> To trembling clients be you mediators:
>   For me, I force not argument a straw,
>   Since that my case is past the help of law.
>
> In vain I rail at opportunity,
> At Time, at Tarquin, and uncheerful night;
> In vain I cavil with mine infamy,
> In vain I spurn at my confirm'd despite;
> This helpless smoke of words doth me no right:
>   The remedy indeed to do me good
>   Is to let forth my foul-defilèd blood.[112]

Such behavior follows no rules; instead, it ends her following rules.

v. The Requirement of Consistent Administration

If rules are to guide conduct, they must of course be administered in a sufficiently consistent manner to permit reasoned and predictable action by those trying to play by the rules. *Measure for Measure* as discussed earlier gives us a clear example of how selective enforcement of law proves treacherous for Claudio yet opportunistic for Angelo.[113] This approach writ large would of course render any putative legal system incoherent as a set of rules for human guidance.

vi. The Prohibition of Retroactive Abuse

Measure for Measure also shows us how abuse of retroactive application of law can undermine a putative legal system. The laws

---

[112] William Shakespeare, *Lucrece*, 1016-1029, Stephen Orgel and A.R. Braunmuller, eds., (NY: Penguin Books, 2002) (hereafter *Lucrece*).

[113] *See* Section IV(C) above.

selectively applied in this play were arguably also retroactive ones. Reviving these sexual behavior laws that had "slept"[114] and suddenly applying them to all would effectively violate the principle that rules may not be impossible to perform. Requiring change of past behavior to comply with rules is of course impossible to perform. [115]

vii. The Requirement of Sufficient Stability

The possibility requirement also applies to the present stability of the legal system. Even without selective enforcement, retroactive abuse, and patently impossible rules, one may effectively have impossible performance where the legal system is in constant flux. In such a situation, the law could not serve as guidance because no course of action could keep up with such flux. If, for example, Cade had succeeded making his mouth "the Parliament of England,"[116] there could have been no law to the extent his mouth was in constant flux.

viii. The Protection of Speech Required by the Previous Seven Requirements

If rules are to serve as guides for conduct, then they must actually fulfill that function. They cannot serve as guides for conduct without a certain degree of implicit freedom of speech. First, there must be speech involved in conveying and implementing the rules. Second there must be speech involved in enforcing the rules. Third, enforcement involves the empirical questions of how to follow the rules and whether the rules are being followed and to what end and effect. There must be speech involved in these continuing empirical questions so long as the rules remain in place. Discontinued

---

[114] *Measure For Measure*, II, ii, 90.
[115] This is not to say that a retroactive rule is always incoherent or impossible to perform in the relevant sense. For example, if a society has consistently operated on the mistaken view that certain property vesting rules were in effect three hundred years ago, a retroactive rule implementing such rules could serve as proper guidance for the living since they could continue to comply with a rule that they had already believed was in place.
[116] *Henry VI*, IV, vii, 13-14.

rules also present continuing empirical questions requiring speech since previously-undiscovered evidence regarding such discontinued rules might present itself at any time. "Rules" suppressing such rules-required speech would therefore contradict the very concept of rules.

Statements involving the law encompass a much wider range than might first be thought, and this effectively requires very broad freedom of expression. For example, a statement such as "Angelo broke the fifty-five mile per hour legal speed limit on Tuesday" of course on its face involves the legal system. This is the case even where there is no actual legal limit and even where there is no speeding by Angelo since it asserts a putative legal claim against him.

Acknowledging this, however, requires acknowledging that an infinite number of other related statements also involve the legal system. These would include, for example, statements such as "Angelo was going x miles per hour," "Angelo's car was travelling x miles per hour," "Angelo was at home in bed on Tuesday," "Angelo never speeds," "Angelo cannot drive," and "Angelo spends his days in seated meditation." These statements would be protected because they all potentially relate to the prosecution or defense of the charge made against Angelo.

Acknowledging this, however, further requires acknowledging that these statements involve the legal system even in the absence of any present charge against Angelo. Prosecutors must have pre-charge freedom to make such a charge and Angelo and others must of course have the freedom to create the record for any such potential charge or its defense. Denying such freedom would restrict the speech required to implement and test the effectiveness of rules regarding speeding and would thus contradict the very notion of such rules.

Of course, acknowledging this also requires acknowledging endless civil law counterparts of this criminal example. For example, the statement "Angelo was looking for chocolate in Europe yesterday" can involve the civil law in endless ways. To the extent "chocolate" has an express or implied meaning under applicable commercial law, the phrase on its face involves the law. However, it could also be a defense to claims that Angelo committed a physical tort in North Carolina yesterday or evidence that he did not sign a quitclaim deed in North Carolina yesterday. Again, no present tort or property claim need be asserted for this to be the case since such claims could be asserted at any time. And, again, denying freedom to make such statements would restrict the speech required to implement and test the rules regarding the legal definition of chocolate, the physical torts in questions or the execution of quitclaim deeds and would thus, again, contradict the very notion of such rules.

Acknowledging this, of course requires acknowledging that very little (if any) expression exists independently of the law.[117] Acknowledging this requires acknowledging the broad degree of freedom of expression required for the governance by rules[118] even in

---

[117] As Borges puts it, "[I]n the human languages there is no proposition that does not imply the entire universe; to say *the tiger* is to say the tigers that begot it, the deer and turtles devoured by it, the grass on which the deer fed, the earth that was mother to the grass, the heaven that gave birth to the earth." Jorge Luis Borges, "The God's Script" in *Labyrinths*, L.A. Murillo, tr. (NY: New Directions Books, 2007), 171. The law, of course, is a part of this universe. If, however, interrelation is somehow questionable under a specific formulation, expression can be rephrased to remove all doubt. For example, "I do not like the color of your hair" can be restated as "This American citizen does not like the color of your hair."

[118] This requirement of course does not apply to all verbal or other acts purporting to be expression. Where "expression" on its face contradicts or does not involve the freedom of expression required for governance by rules, such "expression" may be restricted without contradicting the notion of rules. For example, calling a person "faggot!" simply to hurt or insult him is verbal battery. Battery deliberates nothing and therefore on its face cannot play any role in the discussion or analysis of rules. Furthermore, rules permitting such gratuitous battery would sanction chilled expression in the battered. This on its face is of course inconsistent with the freedom of speech required for the governance of rules. Fictional entities also require different analysis. For example, since corporations are legal fictions which can only speak to the extent the law provides, any questions of corporate free speech are necessarily compound questions requiring analysis of whether putative speech is actually corporate speech and, if so, whether such speech is permitted of corporations by the law that creates and empowers them. If the corporation cannot speak under such analysis, this has no effect on net expression. Corporations can only speak through others and the speech of others (such as shareholders, officers and employees of the corporation) is not muted by the corporation's inability to speak.

the absence of provisions such as the First Amendment.[119] This of course requires acknowledging that all legal systems must permit broad freedom of expression even in the absence of written requirements to such effect.[120]

Thus, Shakespeare allows his "fools" to play the chorus even where "wiser" men would not. The Fool in *King Lear*, for example, freely reminds King Lear of the foolishness of submitting himself to the power of his thankless daughters Regan and Goneril while rejecting his loyal daughter Cordelia. Thus, the Fool remarks even to a king, "Thou shouldst not have been old till thou hadst been wise."[121] Feste in *Twelfth Night, or, What You Will* [hereafter *Twelfth Night*] similarly freely notes that foolery ". . . does walk about the orb like the sun; it shines everywhere."[122] In *Twelfth Night*, he also freely proclaims, "I say there is no darkness but ignorance. . . ."[123] Touchstone, though a duplicitous and pedantic fool, still serves as a good "touchstone" against which others may measure their purity in *As You Like It*.[124]

---

[119] Compare *The Federalist* No. 84 (Alexander Hamilton) setting forth Hamilton's reasons why a bill of rights is unnecessary and even potentially dangerous.

[120] One might argue that this line of argument proves too much. For example, espionage is a rule-governed activity. Does that mean that CIA agents, for example, are therefore free to speak publicly about whatever they do and whatever they find? Of course not—such freedom would contradict the very rules of their profession. However, the epistemological and other concerns we have noted would require their freedom to speak to the extent consistent with such rules. Some might respond, "Then what about a law requiring everyone to be a 'Y' which is defined as one who always keeps strict silence?" Would not speaking violate the inherent rules of that "game" and therefore effectively deny freedom of expression to everyone? However, again, such a "law" is simply not possible. Rules cannot be implemented, enforced or followed without speech. It would not help to modify the law to provide for "strict silence except to the extent required to implement, enforce or follow the law." What falls under that caveat is itself subject to interpretation, implementation and compliance which of course requires the very freedom of expression it would suppress.

[121] *King Lear, op. cit.*, I, v 41-42.

[122] William Shakespeare, *Twelfth Night, or, What you Will*, III, i 38-39, Stephen Orgel and A.R. Braunmuller, eds., (NY: Penguin Books, 2002) (hereafter *Twelfth Night*).

[123] *Id.*, act 4, sc. 2, lines 42-43.

[124] See Harold Bloom, *Shakespeare: The Invention of the Human*, (NY: Riverhead Books, 1998), 218-221.

ix. The Equal Protection Required by the Previous Eight Requirements

Since governance by rules requires freedom of speech to the extent noted above, commensurate equal protection must follow hand in hand for those entitled to freedom of speech. To the extent disparate treatment limits protected speech, governance by rules inherently limits such disparate treatment. For example, a rule-governed society could not lawfully segregate school systems based on an arbitrary factor such as skin color. Separating students and teachers on such a basis clearly interferes with the free flow of ideas and therefore cannot legitimately occur within a rule-based society. That is not to say, of course, that such a practice cannot physically occur in a given society otherwise governed by law. We unfortunately know that such a practice can and has occurred. Yet, where it has occurred, the practice cannot be lawful (even if the "inferior" race accepts it) because it violates the inherent restraint of governance by rules. Shakespeare understands this well: his fools such as Feste, Touchstone and Lear's Fool are allowed to mix freely with all classes of society.

x. The Due Process Required by the Previous Nine Requirements

Meaningful equal protection and freedom of speech cannot of course exist without due process protections. Thus, governance by rules also requires sufficient due process protections to guarantee such freedom of speech and equal protection. Procedural due process is also required by the very nature of governance by rules. Without such procedural due process guarantees, rules implode as internalized guides for individual conduct because the consequences of compliance (and even what constitutes compliance itself) become uncertain. Without such procedural due process, one becomes a Desdemona[125] subject to condemnation no matter what

---

[125] Desdemona is murdered by her husband, Othello, who erroneously believes she has been unfaithful to him. *See* William Shakespeare, *The Tragedy of Othello, the Moor of*

one does. This is not rule-governed activity under any meaningful sense of the term.

VI. CONCLUSION

With Shakespeare's help, we can thus see a clearer picture of the law and its inherent restraints shorn of the false bravado of a Richard III and the false pieties of an Angelo. Although Shakespeare helps us see how command-theory positivism, prediction-theory accounts of the law, and the natural law accounts explored do not stand scrutiny, he also helps us see how the concept of governance by rules has at least ten inherent restraints which prohibit much mischief.[126] Though not from Moses, this semiotic decalogue demands its Nurembergs.

I would like to thank Prof. Michael Kent Curtis and Dr. Harold Brown for their helpful thoughts and comments on this article.

Venice, Stephen Orgel and A.R. Braunmuller, eds., (NY: Penguin Books, 2002).

[126] To the extent these inherent restraints morally fail, at least two further safeguards apply. First, the substantial acceptance requirement always applies and substantial acceptance will by definition cease when the governed find a legal system too dissolute for their continued acceptance. Tyrannical force may continue to be used when such acceptance ceases, but such force is not law and will hopefully face its Nuremberg. Law requires governance by rules, and such governance requires internalizing rules, a requirement no longer met when rules are rejected by the governed. Second, despite what others may do, individuals can of course refuse to obey immoral law.

HONOR, DIGNITY, AND THE *SUMMUM BONUM*: KANT'S RETRIBUTIVISM IN CONTEXT

Jacob M. Held

The following essay is ambitious in intent. My goal is no less than to put Kant's retributivism in the context of his practical philosophy as a whole with specific reference to the concepts of honor, dignity, and the *summum bonum* (highest good). Although my ambition is great my expectations are more modest. I am hoping only that the reader, once progressing through this essay, is able to appreciate the depth and breadth of Kant's practical philosophy and how his retributive theory of punishment is but one inseparable strand of a tightly woven tapestry.

There is much more to Kant's account of punishment than a cursory glance, or even focused reading, of the often cited passages provides. If one remains only with these passages one may be proffered an account of what retribution is, namely, giving to a criminal punishment proportionate to the heinousness of his crime merely because he deserves it. One may even get a glimpse into how Kant calculates desert, namely, proportionality in relation to respect and dignity. But what would be lacking is an understanding of why it is necessary to punish criminals merely because they deserve it. This is a problem for Kant specifically, but also retributive theories of punishment generally. If an answer cannot be offered, then retribution will look no different than revenge.

When retribution is generally treated in analytic philosophy it is dealt with as a matter of proportionate response to some wrongdoing. It is assumed that you punish wrongdoers because they are wrongdoers, and you do so in a way such that the punishment "fits" the crime. The scholarship often then lingers on the determination of "fit." Thus, the questions are asked: How do you determine the severity of a crime? and How do you calculate a proportionately severe punishment? *Mens rea*, culpability, responsibility and other issues may be thrown in for good measure, but the structure of the debate is pretty constant. Then, whoever is asking the questions proffers their responses, which are sure to incite a response from another scholar who has found an inconsistency or other problem with the original proposal, and so on and so on. This procedure is helpful in clarifying some thoughts we might have on retribution.[1] Unfortunately, the debate at this point begins to lose the forest for the trees. The purpose of retribution is lost in light of trying to figure out how to administer it. However, if retribution is ensconced in a natural law tradition which maintains a fundamental respect for dignity and desire to recompense its unjust loss, then to try and administer such a policy in a legal system that has been divested of any natural law presuppositions will be doomed to failure. This is the case we find when current theorists try to rationalize a retributive schema against the backdrop of an ostensibly positivistic legal system. All claims to "just desert" seem arbitrary, and are so as long as the natural law, natural right background is dismissed or disregarded. A more comprehensive treatment of retribution should begin at the role of punishment within a system of right. It is this background that Kant's philosophy of right provides, and so it is towards Kant that we must turn in order to better grasp the depth and breadth of retribution.

When I first asked the question, why is Kant so insistent that criminals must be punished, I was not sure that I would even find an answer. What I found was an answer to the existential quandary of wherefrom the value of human existence comes. The answer lies with dignity, as anyone familiar with Kant could have predicted. But what was not foreseeable was how dignity becomes ensconced in talk of our highest good and not only our faith that this is achievable

---

[1] For good representative pieces on retribution and its problems in this context see: H. L. A. Hart, *Punishment and Responsibility* (New York: Oxford, 1968); Robert Nozick, "Retributive Punishment," in *Readings in Philosophy of Law*, edited by John Arthur and William Shaw (Englewood Cliffs: Prentice Hall, 1984); Russ Shafer-Landau, "The Failure of Retributivism," *Philosophical Studies* 82 (1996); John Cottingham, "Varieties of Retribution," *The Philosophical Quarterly*, Vol. 29, No. 116 (July, 1979); Nigel Walker, "Even More Varieties of Retribution," *Philosophy* 74 (1999); and John Wilson, "The Purpose of Retribution," *Philosophy* Vol. 58, No. 226 (Oct., 1983).

in the afterlife, or the kingdom of ends, but how our social practices, namely justice, right, and even punishment, are analogues for bringing this about in the phenomenal world. In this regard Kant often speaks of honor. It will be through the concept of honor that one can begin to see how retribution fits into a general theory of right, a theory predicated on dignity and respect as exemplified and reinforced through social recognition manifested via social practices. Kant's ethics are often treated as disconnected from life as lived. But his practical philosophy, when taken as a whole, is nothing short of an answer to the question of how we ought to value human life, and how this value can be made manifest in the social world through our shared social practices. Kant's practical philosophy values our lives and offers the guidelines according to which we may live praiseworthy lives. Kant's practical philosophy is nothing short of an attempt to legitimate and motivate a worldview wherein the value of human life is secured by a moral social order in an attempt to make this world livable, that is, worth living in and worthy of humanity. If one adds to this an understanding of our highest good and how its attainment redeems our earthly existence, then it can be seen how justice, as a commitment to ensure wickedness gets punished and honor rewarded, secures the closest possible analogue to the highest good in this realm. Our earthly state can begin to approximate the kingdom of ends. Thus Kant's ethics ties into his philosophy of right and gives retribution meaning as a means to secure rightful honor in this life. Unfortunately, this aspect of Kant is often lost in the scholarship as debates get centered on minutiae. Yet, bringing this aspect of Kant back into the discussion of retribution both provides a fuller explanation of Kant's philosophy of right and theory of punishment while also contextualizing retribution and so giving it a more comprehensive account.

However, this essay is neither an apologetic for Kant or retributivism; it is an exercise in exegesis. Various conclusions are suggested and could be drawn from what follows. But one that seems most fitting is that retribution is a part of a worldview that adheres to the dignity of the human being, the necessity to respect this, and that the role of the state is to promote and reinforce this value. With regard to Kant, retributivism may only be adequately understood once one has reconstructed his worldview. Kant's practical philosophy is no less than an existential response to the human condition. Retribution is part and parcel of this worldview insofar as punishment respects persons by honoring the meritorious and humiliating the wicked, and in so doing makes the world a reflection of the ideal moral order, the kingdom of ends, where one's happiness is secured in direct proportion to one's worthiness of being happy, or virtue. In fact, punishment is fundamental since it would be impossible to honor the honorable and maintain the integrity of a system premised on the notion that one's happiness is in accord with one's deservingness if the wicked went unpunished. Retribution, as part of such an all encompassing system can only make sense if one maintains the worldview that sees value as fundamental to a meaningful life and the role of the state as reinforcing this value by means of social practices.

WHAT DOES RETRIBUTION DO?

Understanding retribution is not about grasping the truth value of the propositions that comprise a particular argument or assessing the relative strength of their connection to a conclusion. Retribution is not about being able to prove beyond a doubt how to calculate, apportion, and distribute just deserts. Retribution is about establishing a moral order, namely, evenness between victim and victimizer, thus affirming the worth of persons. Retribution is a symbolic exchange and therefore it is all about context; what is being exchanged, by whom, and for what purpose. Looking back to cultures that were unabashedly retributive and seeing how they operated will provide a window onto how Kant attempted to reproduce this type of moral ordering as an answer to the question of how human life ought to be valued and how society ought to be organized in accordance with and for the purpose of promoting and reproducing this order. If one wants to understand Kantian retribution, one would do well to begin with honor.

In William Ian Miller's latest book, *Eye for an Eye*, the reader is given a historical account of *lex talionis*, the law of retaliation. In this work, Miller explores "the talion," which according to Miller, is about a repayment in kind. The talion is more than simply blood lust or a desire for revenge; it is about evenness, leveling the scales of justice, paying back a criminal for the wrong they committed as well as paying back, or making whole, the victim, which may be a singular victim or society as a whole.[2] Thus, retribution is about much more than the simplistic formula of an eye for an eye, it is the means by which value is measured, wrongs adjudicated, victims restored to moral wholeness and the social fabric mended. "[T]he talion cuts deeper … For what it means to do is measure and value *us*."[3]

Miller's basic claim is: if justice is retributive, then it is also restorative. As one scholar notes, "The purpose of retribution … is to compensate the injured, an idea contained in the meaning of 'retribution.'"[4] With respect to the distinction between retribution making the victim whole, and retaliation, or the infliction of harm on the offender, one scholar points out that wholeness is measured not merely in terms of quantifiable, clearly fungible goods such as pain, healing, and loss of time, but also intangibles like degradation.[5] The introduction of degradation, a loss of social standing, introduces moral damages into the equation in a way that demands that if these are to be paid back, and if the victim is to be restored to moral wholeness, then retribution must contain within it a symbolic

---

[2] For a contemporary account of retribution see Christopher Bennett, "The Varieties of Retributive Experience," *The Philosophical Quarterly* Vol. 52, No. 207 (Apr. 2002), 145-163.

[3] William Ian Miller, *Eye for an Eye* (New York: Cambridge University Press, 2006), ix.

[4] John Wilson, "The Purpose of Retribution," *Philosophy* 58, No. 226 (Oct., 1983), 521-22.

[5] B. Sharon Byrd, "Justice and Talionis," *S'vara: A Journal of Philosophy, Law, and Judaism* 2, No. 1 (1991), p. 66.

lowering of the pretensions of the wrongdoer, that is, humiliation. Although one cannot make it as though a victim has not suffered a loss, one can repay him for those things that remuneration can fix, and insofar as the crime is also a moral affront punishment can affirm his worth as a person and the merit of the norms that have been violated. The fact that honor or loss of moral status is not quantifiable in the same way as physical harm, or loss of time or property does not make it any less an affront. In fact, the notion that one's interests are exhausted by physical goods and so harms are only compensable when measurable in material terms is contentious and paints a very shallow understanding of the contours and worth of human life. If some affronts are moral, then reparations can only be dealt with in terms of a moral exchange.

Acknowledging evenness or restoration as the goal of retributive punishment does raise the problem of adjudication. The scales of justice can be recognized to be askew without there being an obvious way to realign them, especially if they are calibrated by way of moral values. A retributive theory of justice is approximate at best. Retributivists must give up certainty. But what system of justice can guarantee this? Miller states, "There has to be some play in the joints that allows for imaginative and creative restorations of equilibrium or for dealing practically with a reality that is always more complex than even the precisest of rules can get a grip on."[6] Calculations will of necessity be sloppy, but they will get the job done in a justifiable way, and since— as will be claimed below— the job being done is necessary, there is not much more than can be asked but that it is done as well as possible. So even if damages may not be calculable in discreet increments in the way monetary awards are afforded for property damages that does not mean that values like honor and dignity are not fungible in the sense of open to exchange via some symbolic transfer. Consider one of Miller's examples.

One of the most illustrative of Miller's examples is King Aethelberht's laws during his reign in Kent from 590-616 A.D. These

---

[6] Miller, *Eye for an Eye*, 6

laws are claimed to be the earliest of their kind written in English. King Aethelberht's laws enumerate myriad offenses from breaking arms, legs, severing feet, toes, or fingers, as well as the generative limb, to lesser damages such as grabbing hair or a punch to the nose. Each of these offenses is followed by a price to be paid as remuneration. For the grabbing of hair, 2 and one half schillings, for a severed foot, 50 schillings, the generative limb is worth three *wergelds,* that is, three times the price of the worth of a full person, and so forth.[7] This can seem simplistic and in virtue of its simplicity cruel— to disparage the human body into nothing more than a list of prices is prima facie repugnant. But, in measuring the value of a lost limb, appendage, organ, or even life one is not reducing life to simple currency; rather one is attempting to translate into fungible goods what is not so clearly fungible, to repay values like lost honor with values like coinage. Restoring one to wholeness, especially when honor is on the line is a job one can approximate at best. But if restoration is to be accomplished one must approximate. Exchange is a symbolic transfer and just as it works with monetary value, so it does with moral value as well.

Currency is the means of exchange but it far from exhausts the symbolism of what is being transferred. Consider the banal example of an eye for an eye. If it is made clear that the penalty for wrongfully taking my eye—which Aethelberht prices at 50 schillings—is that I can claim yours, we may say it is simply a matter of deterrence. People will be more careful about putting out eyes. This may be true. But what is affirmed above and beyond any deterrent effect of the law is the fact that if after you take my eye I can claim a right to yours, then I am effectively pricing my eye at what you would pay to keep yours. Miller summarizes, "The talion structures the bargaining situation to simulate the hypothetical bargain that would have been struck had I been able to set the price of my eye *before* you took it."[8] You will as a result value my eye as much as you value

[7] *Ibid*, pp. 113-115.
[8] *Ibid*, pp. 49-50.

yours. Your reluctance to hand over your eye proves its value and hence by substitution the value of mine, and so affirms our equal worth as persons. You now value me as much as you value yourself. The talion forces a sympathetic bond.[9] In fact, one might go even further and claim that beyond mere sympathy the talion reinforces respect by forcing the recognition of equality between members of society. As one scholar so aptly states: "Tit-for-tat treatment is a simple … way of getting an individual to face up to the question of what rules he really wants to be in force: if he thinks it proper to do such-and-such, then he must think it proper to have such-and-such done back to him."[10] An eye for an eye is about sympathy and the recognition of a moral order affirming the equal worth of persons.

Situating the talion in honor cultures helps clarify much. Firstly, retribution is not merely about being backward looking. Although one's punishment is determined by one's past misdeeds, the restorative aspect of payback looks beyond the damage done to a present and future circumstance in which the situation is returned to even, or repaired. Through the affirmative aspect of punishment one is looking also to the future. As Miller notes: "[L]ooking to the future quality of your honor … meant that you really did have to look backward now and then …"[11] We cannot make things right if we do not know what went wrong, but that does not mean we must focus myopically on the past without reference to the future. Retribution is both backward looking insofar as it respects the past, and forward looking insofar as it seeks to remedy past grievances by restoring future value. Retribution is thus not simply about dealing out just deserts for past wrongs, but also recognizing and affirming the worth of persons through public ritual.

Although, as Miller notes, contemporary talk about dignity implies it is inviolable and beyond price, and Kant in fact distinguished directly between something having a price (*Preis*) and a dignity

---

[9] See B. Sharon Byrd, "Justice and Talionis," 65.
[10] Wilson, "The Purposes of Retribution," 524.
[11] Miller, *Eye for an Eye*, 23.

(*Würde*) or absolute inner worth (*Wert*),[12] the honor cultures with which Miller deals spoke an ostensibly different language: "Everything is compensable."[13] Although this gives the appearance of pricing people and thereby denying them their worth or dignity, the opposite is the case. By recognizing all things to be compensable the jurists of whom Miller writes were affirming that justice as evenness demands a metric of equivalences so that affronts to one's honor, that is, one's worth can be restored through retributive justice. There was a price for everything, because everything had a value and needed to be fungible in a common idiom of exchange. Their price for a human life was *wergeld*, or man-price. This price measured one's legal rank and dictated how much one's kin must be compensated in the event of one's untimely death: the higher the rank, the higher the price.[14] One's worth is subsequently measured in terms of what can be exchanged: money. But simply setting a price is not denigrating. Even Kant who adheres inflexibly to the absolute worth of human life, its inherent dignity, sets a man-price on the crime of murder, execution. He may not allow one to pay off their debt in schillings or thalers, but he does demand payment. As an exchange of symbols what is exchanged is not nearly as important as what it stands for, the trinket is a mere placeholder for a value being recognized by a social practice of exchange. If justice is to be meted out, that is, if restoration is to be made, and if crimes are also considered moral affronts, then values must be fungible goods. There must be a way to trade in the symbols of moral value such that the debt of the crime may be paid in full by the punishment. Retributive punishment is encapsulated in a moral framework around and inextricably linked to a discussion of the value of human life, its respectability, and how its value is affirmed through social practices. Putting retribution in this context sheds a great deal of light on Kant.

---

[12] See Immanuel Kant, *Metaphysics of Morals*, translated and edited by Mary Gregor (Cambridge: Cambridge University Press, 1996), 186 [6:434-5].
[13] Miller, *Eye for an Eye*, 130.
[14] Miller, *Eye for an Eye*, 9.

THE *SUMMUM BONUM*, OR WHY DO WE NEED RETRIBUTION?

Retribution is about human worth and how it is recognized in the social world. What punishment does is not seek to value us, for our value lies in our freedom, in our inherent human dignity, but it seeks to affirm, reaffirm, and reinforce that value when a wrongdoing has denigrated it. Insofar as the law is able to do this the state makes the world a place befitting and even worthy of humanity. The fundamental concept for grasping retribution in this context is dignity, the worth of persons. So it is with dignity that we begin our discussion of Kant.

The clearest way to understand what Kant is trying to effect by means of his moral philosophy, is the creation of a worldview wherein human life is given a value in light of the fact that empirical, phenomenal reality appears to be law governed and determined. If one were to reduce the human being to merely another law governed creature in the order of creation his life would lack all value, it would just be one more mechanism. But to postulate freedom frees the human being from the phenomenal world and grants him noumenal status, that is, status beyond the law governed reality where causality loses its hold, where human beings are determiners of their own actions, where they are free and thus can have a value in and of themselves and a metric against which they may be judged and valued. As J. G. Fichte would so elegantly put it, "When you think yourself as free, you are forced to think your freedom under a law; and when you think this law, you are forced to think yourself as free ... the first article of faith is: *I am genuinely free*; for it paves the path into the intelligible world, and secures for us there a sure footing."[15] This view of human life is predicated on certain practi-

---

[15] Johann Gottlieb Fichte, "System of the Science of Ethics (Das System der Sittlichlehre nach den Principien der Wissenschaftslehre): First Part – Deduction of the Principle of Ethics (1798)," translated by David W. Wood, in *German Idealism: An Anthology and Guide*, edited by Brian O'Connor and Georg G. Mohr (Chicago: University of Chicago

cal postulates, most importantly, the existence of freedom. We are allowed to attribute to ourselves freedom insofar as we consider ourselves as noumenal beings, that is, beings not determined by the law of causality as are all phenomena, but rather outside of phenomena and so beyond the law of causality.[16] This belief is warranted once we recognize that we can give ourselves laws or commands, ethical imperatives, and follow them, that is, act according to self-imposed laws and not merely abide by the laws of nature. We are autonomous. Kant thus offers an answer, one might even anachronistically call "existential," to a very real problem: how do we view and value human life in a Newtonian mechanized world where we appear as just another mechanism? The answer is to attribute to us a twofold nature, and it is our noumenal self from which our value arises.

The value of people stems from their status as rational beings, a status that allows us to postulate freedom, and people are valuable as the possessors of freedom. "I say now: every being that cannot act otherwise than *under the idea of freedom* is just because of that really free in a practical respect ... I assert that to every rational being having a will we must necessarily lend the idea of freedom also, under which alone he acts."[17] But freedom itself cannot be proven, for it cannot be experienced. Rather it is through our awareness of our capacity to give ourselves a moral law to which we are bound in virtue of being rational that we are able to postulate our freedom. Our ability to give ourselves the moral law demonstrates our freedom and our freedom makes our adherence to the moral law possible.[18] Insofar as people are free they are the wellspring of value, that is, they are that which is valuable in itself for everything else in this world is valued merely as a means to a further end. People,

---

Press, 2006), 121-2.

[16] Cf. Immanuel Kant, *Groundwork of the Metaphysics of Morals*, translated and edited by Mary Gregor, (Cambridge: Cambridge University Press, 1997), 61-2 [4:457-458].

[17] Kant, *Groundwork of the Metaphysics of Morals*, 53 [4:448].

[18] Cf. Immanuel Kant, *Critique of Practical Reason*, translated and edited by Mary Gregor (Cambridge: Cambridge University Press, 1997), 26-27 [5:29-30]; *Metaphysics of Morals*, p. 14 [6:221].

as free, are valued in virtue of being free. Kant declares. "*Honeste vive* (live honourably), i.e. truly honour what universally has worth. What necessarily has a worth for everyone possesses dignity, and he who possesses it has inner worth."[19] Likewise, "that which constitutes the condition under which alone something can be an end in itself has not merely a relative worth, that is, a price, but an inner worth, that is, dignity ... an unconditional, incomparable worth; and the word *respect* alone provides a becoming expression for the estimate of it that a rational being must give."[20] Insofar as human beings possess dignity, they are owed respect. Respect is a moral relation between us and ourselves, and other dignified beings, and it is a relation demanded by our status as dignified, free beings. "There rests ... a duty regarding the respect that must be shown to every other human being."[21] Respect is shown through our actions, it is averred through our statements and sanctions and it is ultimately enshrined in our laws as respectful of the universal law of freedom, that is, respect for the freedom of all rational beings. Respect is demonstrated through our behaviors, namely, respectful relations between people, and these are often exhibited through cultural practices and made explicit through law.

In Kant's ethics respect for oneself and others is shown via adherence to the categorical imperative. In two of the formulations we are shown how living rationally, that is morally, we demonstrate both respect for ourselves and respect for others, and we are also shown how violating the moral law is both disrespectful not only to other people but also to ourselves. Thus we can affront the dignity of others and also shame ourselves when we fail to uphold the moral law. In fact, shame and humiliation go hand in hand with respect when it comes to the moral law, which we ought to defer to and revere in its perfection and greatness. "If something represented *as a*

---

[19] Immanuel Kant, *Lectures on Ethics*, edited by Peter Heath and J. B. Schneewind, translated by Peter Heath (Cambridge: Cambridge University Press, 1997), 246 [29:631].

[20] Kant, *Groundwork of the Metaphysics of Morals*, 42 [4:435-436].

[21] Kant, *The Metaphysics of Morals*, 209 [6:462].

determining ground of our will humiliates us in our self-consciousness, it awakens *respect* for itself ..."[22] Since we are not perfectly good wills, but tempted by our inclinations and in fact inherently weakened by our constitution as embodied wills we need to be necessitated to obey the moral law, that is, we need to be forced or helped in order that we might respect ourselves and others and not be shamed before the awesomeness of the moral law. "Respect for the moral law must be regarded as a positive though indirect effect of the moral law on feeling insofar as the law weakens the hindering influence of the inclinations by humiliating self-conceit, and must therefore be regarded as a subjective ground of activity ... as the incentive to compliance with the law ..."[23] The categorical imperative, or the laws we give to ourselves, provide rules by which we direct our activities so that we might approximate better a moral life. They do so by necessitating our moral behavior since we are naturally inclined to act contrary to the moral law given our dual nature as both noumenal and phenomenal. "All practical rules consist in an imperative which says what I ought to do. They are meant to signify that a free action, possible through myself, would necessarily occur, if reason were to have total control over my will."[24]

Yet one might wonder why humans would strive to be moral at all. Kant's moral theory demands strict obedience and provides no promise of leading to an affectively happy life. Why not be immoral, that is, live according to our inclinations and be happy? Why not shun a rigorous morality for something more akin to eudaimonia or simple satisfaction, contentment, or a life of ease? If we are not motivated to be good in some sense, then there is no point to demand us to do what we have absolutely no inclination or desire to do. All ethical theories will have in them a moral psychology explaining how to implement the theory being proposed. Kant is no exception. Kant recognizes the drive to be happy as inherent in the human con-

---

[22] Kant, *Critique of Practical Reason*, 64 [5:74].
[23] *Ibid*, 68 [5:79].
[24] Kant, *Lectures on Ethics*, p. 229 [29:605].

dition, but he cannot nor will he cede dignity and respectability to mere satisfaction. Obedience to the moral law gives us worth, happiness will have to take care of itself. But Kant is willing to help it along.

Kant notes that practical reason, as all faculties of reason, is motivated by an interest, that is, an end or goal it seeks to bring about; reason is teleological. For practical reason the end or goal it seeks to bring about is the *summum bonum*, or the highest good. Kant defines the highest good as happiness in accordance with virtue. "Virtue and happiness together constitute possession of the highest good in a person, and happiness distributed in exact proportion to morality (as the worth of a person and his worthiness to be happy) constitutes the *highest good* of a possible world …"[25] Likewise, "Virtue is the greatest worth of the person, but our state must also be worth wishing for. The greatest worth of one's state is happiness. So virtue combined with happiness is the highest good."[26] That is, we seek to be as happy as we deserve to be given the degree to which we live a moral life. We want what we deserve. We want the happiness we have earned through our moral behavior. This is an end practical reason puts before us, and towards which we strive. "The moral law … also defines for us a final end … and makes it obligatory upon us to strive towards its attainment. This end is the *summum bonum*, as the highest good in the world possible through freedom."[27] This desire, however, is doomed to failure so long as we live in these bodies and on this earth. After all, life is unfair, as our children are so prone to point out, and we do not get what we deserve, namely the rewards we earn through good behavior. Conversely the wicked do not get what they deserve, that is righteous punishment. Too often the good suffer and the evil thrive. If Kant ended the story here, with a desire to achieve the highest good, a doomed endeavor, the future of hu-

---

[25] Kant, *Critique of Practical Reason*, 93 [5:110].
[26] Kant, *Lectures on Ethics*, 227 [29:600].
[27] Immanuel Kant, "Part Two: Critique of Teleological Judgement," in *The Critique of Judgement*, translated by James Creed Meredith (Oxford: Clarendon Press, 1952), 118.

man existence would be bleak. One might go so far as to say that Kant without the hope of achieving the highest good is a pessimist. Perhaps, the only thing separating Kant from the pessimism of Arthur Schopenhauer is Kant's optimism that happiness in accordance with virtue is possible. But the only way Kant can get here is to look beyond this world.

Since practical reason drives us towards the *summum bonum* we are allowed, that is, it is permissible and perhaps even demanded that we believe it is attainable. "Morality and the expectation of a happiness proportionate to it as its result can at least be thought as possible … .since no one can want to maintain that a worthiness of rational beings in the world to be happy in conformity with the moral law combined with a possession of this happiness proportioned to it is impossible in itself."[28] This requires a leap of faith, a practical faith or pure rational belief. "Faith … is the confidence of attaining a purpose the furthering of which is a duty, but whose achievement is a thing of which we are unable to *perceive* the possibility …"[29] In order to secure the possibility of the highest good Kant offers two practical postulates, the belief in an immortal soul, and the belief in a God. The soul grants us the possibility of perfection, that is, given infinite time I can live a perfectly good life, one entirely in accord with reason, especially if it is severed from this body full of inclinations. Secondly, this soul will be as happy as it deserves to be since God, as just, will make it the case that people are rewarded according to desert. God and a soul allow us to achieve our highest good.[30] Kant concludes, "Only if religion is added … does there also enter the hope of some day participating in happiness to the degree that we have been intent upon not being unworthy of it."[31]

Kant is placing human beings as dignified within a mechanistic world in order to achieve nothing short of a synthesis between the

---

[28] Kant, *Critique of Practical Reason*, 99, 120 [5:119, 144].

[29] Kant, "Part Two: Critique of Teleological Judgement," in *The Critique of Judgement*, 146 .

[30] Cf. Kant, *Critique of Practical Reason*, 102-108 [5:122-130] *passim*.

[31] Kant, *Critique of Practical Reason*, 108 [5:130].

phenomenal world of law-governed brute reality and the noumenal world of free, dignified human life. Kant has constructed a worldview and it is from within this worldview that one must look at punishment and retribution. It may seem as if we are a long way from retribution in the penal, earthly sense, but this metaphysico-religious background sets the scene for the earthly desire for, necessity of, and attempts at justice, namely, rewards and punishments in accord with moral worth. As Kant notes: "the sovereignty of the good principle is attainable, so far as men can work toward it, only through the establishment and spread of a society whose task and duty it is rationally to impress these laws in all their scope upon the entire human race."[32] Kant is interested in no less than proposing and implementing a just order on earth, one that abides by and approximates the ideal moral order of the kingdom of ends, that is, a heaven on earth.

WHAT DOES KANT'S RETRIBUTIVISM DO?

If one were to jump headlong into Kant's philosophy of punishment one would likely be exposed to a quote such as "If ... he has committed a murder he must *die*. Here there is no substitute that will satisfy justice. There is no *similarity* between life, however wretched it may be, and death, hence no likeness between the crime and the retribution unless death is judicially carried out upon the wrongdoer, although it must still be freed from any mistreatment that could make the humanity in the person suffering it into something abominable."[33] Thus one is presented with the fairly standard and straightforward notion that murderers deserve death; the only fitting measure of a life is another life. In this simple formulation Kant appears to evince the classical notion of what is usually referred to as *lex talionis*, or what is colloquially referenced as "eye for an eye." In order to respect both victim and criminal, people should be pun-

---

[32] Immanuel Kant, *Religion within the Limits of Reason Alone*, translated by Theodore M. Greene (New York: Haper Torchbooks, 1960), 86.

[33] Kant, *The Metaphysics of Morals*, 106 [6:333].

ished because they deserve it and in proportion to their wrongdoing. With respect to this simplistic formulation, the focus is put on proportionality; making sure that the criminal receives a punishment equivalent to the harm they have caused. A great deal of literature on retribution focuses on this aspect of the theory, namely, determining proportionate punishment. But concentrating here is infelicitous insofar as it ignores the most important element of retribution, not how one determines proportionate punishments, but why one *must* do so. The above quote communicates more than just a formula for measuring and distributing punishment. What is also included is the moral demand that punishment must be meted out in proportion to desert. Kant emphasizes: "The law of punishment is a categorical imperative, and woe to him who crawls through the windings of eudaemonism in order to discover something that releases the criminal from punishment ... for justice ceases to be justice if it can be bought for any price whatsoever."[34] Punishment must be done, and straying from the demands of justice is disastrous, not because it will lead to greater suffering, but because it disparages the values upon which a system of justice must be based, namely, dignity and respect. It is this warning that Kant offers when he declares "woe to him who crawls through the winding of eudaemonism," that is most instructive. Kant is evincing his concern that seeking out and acting only for materialistic goods is a path that leads to degradation, to the dismissal of dignity and the value of human life for mere comfort. As Miller iterates near the end of his study; "[A]ssuming the role of defender of honor culture ... those obscene amounts we pay to grant ourselves extra unproductive years bespeak less of our virtue than our vice, less of our commitment to dignity than to a lack thereof. We are so afraid of death and pain that we will bankrupt our grandchildren's generation to add on more useless years at the butt-end of our days than we know what to do with. Cowardice, lust, luxury, slothful ease. There is no honor in them at all. We price ourselves

---

[34] *Ibid,* 105 [6: 331-2].

more highly as pleasure machines than as working beings."[35] Retributivism speaks a different language, one in which Kant is fluent. Retributivism is enshrined in a system of right (*Recht*) premised on dignity and respect.

English of course does not have a perfect analogue for the German "Recht" so it is translated as "right," and often conflated with "law." But *Recht* has a connotation above and beyond law; it carries a moral tenor indicating beyond simple laws the moral justification upon which those laws are predicated. *Recht* indicates a moral background against which positive law can be legitimated and adjudicated. This distinction between right and law is in line with the Latin distinction between *Ius* and *Lex*. The distinction between *ius talionis* and *lex talionis*—too often taken as synonymous for "law of retaliation"—is of great importance. Kant uses the former when referencing the moral justification of retributive punishment, not the latter.[36] His use is indicative of his adherence to a distinction that goes back to Cicero.[37] *Ius* or right applies to the pre-legal moral rationale or justification for a particular positivistic law, or *lex*. Right precedes law, that is, the moral law is prior to and in fact provides justification for positive law. Given Kant's familiarity with Cicero it is fair to claim that his intentional use of *ius* and *lex* in contexts suggestive of Cicero's own usage demonstrates an adherence to this distinction.[38] Thus *ius talionis*, the right of retaliation, implies a moral criterion, whereas *lex* when translated or interpreted as "law" carries a positivistic overtone suggesting that *lex* are merely the imperfect manifestation of *ius*. So if one wishes to get to the heart of Kant's theory of punishment, one must begin with *ius talionis*.

---

[35] Miller, *Eye for an Eye*, 57.

[36] Cf. Kant, *The Metaphysics of Morals*, 105 [6:332] for simply one example.

[37] See the entry under *Ius* in the "Text and Translation" section of *Cicero: On the Commonwealth and On the Laws*, edited by James E. G. Zetzel (Cambridge: Cambridge University Press, 1999), xl. "*Ius* also has the connotation of 'justice' —that is, the broader principles of equity and morality which a legal system is supposed to embody."

[38] Manfred Kuehn has noted how impactful Cicero was on Kant's thinking. See: *Kant: A Biography* (Cambridge: Cambridge University Press, 2001).

According to Kant, right (*ius*) is: "… the sum of the conditions under which the choice of one can be united with the choice of another in accordance with a universal law of freedom."[39] Right is a relation between persons concerning external actions and the preservation of each person's freedom, and "[f]reedom (independence from being constrained by another's choice), insofar as it can coexist with the freedom of every other in accordance with a universal law, is the only original right belonging to every man by virtue of his humanity."[40] Insofar as people are free, that is, autonomous, they are possessors of dignity and are thus to be afforded respect. Right is codified respect. Kant continues, "Any action is *right* if it can coexist with everyone's freedom in accordance with a universal law, or if on its maxim the freedom of choice of each can coexist with everyone's freedom in accordance with a universal law."[41] So people can do as they please so long as they do not impair another's freedom to do likewise. Right is a moral relation that must be upheld so long as freedom is to be preserved and by means of its preservation dignity averred. Given that a state is "a union of a multitude of human beings under laws of right,"[42] the state has the duty to enforce the universal law of freedom and thus maintain a suitable environment for dignified beings.

If it is the state's duty to uphold the law and thereby relations of right, then it is also the state's duty to enforce the laws. The law, as predicated on the universal law of freedom, is comprised of strict duties and when one's transgression is the violation of a strict duty of right then it is a crime.[43] A crime is thus not merely pragmatically infelicitous but also morally repugnant. Insofar as a crime violates the universal law of freedom it is an affront to one's dignity. "Law is the totality of all our compulsory duties (*leges strictae*) … *Lex* is

---

[39] Kant, *The Metaphysics of Morals*, 24 [6:230].
[40] *Ibid.*, p. 30 [6:237].
[41] *Ibid*, p. 24 [6: 230].
[42] *Ibid*, p. 90 [6:313].
[43] Cf. Kant, *The Metaphysics of Morals*, 16 [6:224].

that to which there are no exceptions."[44] We have a duty to behave lawfully and the state has a duty to uphold the law. Punishment is a categorical imperative. Law is a relation of right dictated by the moral constitution of autonomous agents and the maintenance of that order is the purpose of the law. In this regard, Kant notes that obeying the law is doing what is owed (*debitem*), that is, what can be demanded and expected from one, and "if what [one] does is *less* than the law requires, it is morally *culpable*...The *rightful* effect of what is culpable is *punishment* ..."[45] Punishment is a right, that is, *ius talionis* or the right to retaliation must be upheld insofar as it instantiates a moral relation of respect both for the dignity of the victim and their ability to assert their right to freedom, but also the dignity of the criminal insofar as they are to be held to account for a morally culpable action. The right to retaliation is a moral right, thus to shun it or deviate is to stray from what is morally demanded.

As noted above, Kant maintains that the law of punishment is a categorical imperative. Punishment, thus, is demanded insofar as respect is demanded by all dignified beings. Consider the practical formula of the categorical imperative, the formula of the end in itself: "So act that you use humanity, whether in your own person or in the person of any other, always at the same time as an end, never merely as a means."[46] Herein lay two fundamental concepts for Kant, dignity and respect. All human beings insofar as they are *autonomous* possess inherent dignity. They can decide to act on those principles, or maxims, that correspond with the "moral law" as described by the categorical imperative, or they can act out of selfish desires and self-interest—self-love also appears to be the motive for law breaking

---

[44] Kant, *Lectures on Ethics*, 239, 248 [29:620, 633].

[45] Kant, *The Metaphysics of Morals*, 19 [6:228]. It is clear why one notable scholar sees Kantian retributivism as a form of debt satisfaction or based on a notion of reciprocity. Cf. Jeffrie Murphy, *Kant The Philosophy of Right* (London: Macmillan and Co., Ltd., 1970), 140-149; "Kant's Theory of Criminal Punishment," *Proceedings of the Third International Kant Congress*, ed. Lewis White Beck (Dordrecht-Holland: D. Reidel Publishing Company, 1972), 434-441.

[46] Kant, *Groundwork of the Metaphysics of Morals*, 38 [4:429].

as well—and hence immorally. Each person's capacity to make this choice proves their moral value or dignity, and by virtue of this dignity, persons deserve respect, to be treated always as valuable ends in themselves, and never only as means to someone else's ends.[47] Likewise, the alternative formulation of the categorical imperative, *"act only in accordance with that maxim through which you can at the same time will that it become a universal law,"*[48] evinces again the same principles of respect and dignity. In this case, acting from this principle demonstrates one's ability to give the law to oneself thus demonstrating one's autonomy, one's freedom. To obey the categorical imperative is to respect oneself. The value of human beings stems from their freedom, but is only affirmed, that is, recognized when they behave as free and treat others likewise. These are inflexible requirements since there is no exception to freedom other than slavery and there is no exception from dignity other than degradation. Insofar as slavery and degradation are beneath humanity, they are to be avoided. Straying from the categorical demands of the moral law betrays what it is about being human that is valuable.

As contentious as it may sometimes be, it needs to be asserted that criminals are people too, no matter how wretched. In order to treat the criminal as a human being with dignity, we can only punish him if he has committed a crime, and his punishment must reflect his status as a possessor of dignity. We punish the criminal because it is demanded that he be held accountable for his wrongdoing, to do otherwise is disrespectful to him. Kant states: "Nonetheless I cannot deny all respect to even a vicious man as a human being; I cannot withdraw at least the respect that belongs to him in his quality as a human being, even though by his deeds he makes himself unworthy of it. So there can be disgraceful punishments that dishonor humanity itself (such as quartering a man, having him torn by dogs, cut-

---

[47] In places, such as *The Metaphysics of Morals* [6:329-330] Kant does suggest that one can lose one's dignity and this claim has at times been used to justify or make consistent Kant's respect for persons and his support for the death penalty. This topic is beyond the purview of the current piece.

[48] Kant, *Groundwork of the Metaphysics of Morals*, 31 [4:421].

ting off his nose and ears.)"⁴⁹ Punishment is an overt, publicly sanctioned act determined by the law of freedom, demanded by justice, and bounded by the moral law. The right to retaliate does not negate the worth of the wrongdoer. But as Kant notes, part of the role of the moral law is to humiliate those before it and thus instill in them a feeling of respect for that which is supremely good. The law, as reflective of this moral code will likewise carry with it an element of humiliation. But shame in itself is not demeaning or a denial of one's dignity, in fact, it affirms dignity by holding us accountable to a standard of moral uprightness. Insofar as the law is reflective of the moral law, and the criminal is an autonomous being, the punishment will include in it a necessary element of shame and humiliation. Just as a wrongdoer is humiliated before the moral law itself, so must a criminal be humiliated before the state as a transgressor of the relations of right.

In the moral sphere, respect for the moral law, as the law of one's freedom, or as a legislator in a kingdom of ends is supposed to humble us, that is our self-love is put in check and we are in fact humiliated by the moral law, thus instilling in us a feeling of respect for the law, as well as inspiring obedience. "[T]he moral law unavoidably humiliates every human being when he compares with it the sensible propensity of his nature."⁵⁰ But a system of right is able not simply by means of internal sanction but via external punishment to instill this respect through public humiliation, that is, punishment. Kant states: "In every punishment there is something that (rightly) offends the accused's feeling of honor, since it involves coercion that is unilateral only, so that his dignity as a citizen is suspended, at least in this particular case."⁵¹ Humiliation, loss of honor, and a sense of shame are all part and parcel to Kant's retributivism. The criminal should experience his wrongdoing with

---

⁴⁹ Kant, *Metaphysics of Morals*, 210 [6:463]. Although this raises some other questions since at [6:363] Kant advocates for castration in the cases of rape or pederasty.

⁵⁰ Kant, *Critique of Practical Reason*, 64 [5:76].

⁵¹ Ibid, 130 [6:363 fn].

the same pangs of conscience that one ought to feel when one violates the moral law; a sense of shame before that which demands respect. This connection between morality and legality is implicit within Kant's theory of right. Humiliation and shame are the counterparts to honor, a notion that also occurs throughout Kant's practical works. It is honor that explains the placement of the individual within a greater system of values, expressed and reinforced through the social practice of punishment.

The notion of honor occurs sporadically throughout Kant's practical philosophy. With respect to death as an honorable punishment Kant makes reference to the example of seditious and rebellious activities perpetrated by both a scoundrel, one out for one's own good, and an honorable revolutionary, that is, one who mistakenly but for principled reasons seeks the overthrow of the government. In terms of what each of these perpetrators deserves as punishment Kant references honor. If both were captured and offered a choice between the death penalty or hard labor Kant states, "the man of honor would choose death, and the scoundrel convict labor … for the man of honor is acquainted with something that he values even more highly than life, namely *honor*, while the scoundrel considers it better to live in shame than not to live at all."[52] A scoundrel prizes a shameful life whereas an honorable man prizes an honorable death. One values life merely for its duration, its brute material satisfaction, the other values what life symbolizes, his freedom, his dignity. For Kant, "It is better to sacrifice life than to forfeit morality. It is not necessary to live, but it is necessary that, so long as we live, we do so honourably."[53]

Another place in which honor makes a notable appearance is in Kant's discussion of slander. The wealthy man who slanders another must not merely pay a fine, but be humiliated in the process. "A fine, for example, imposed for a verbal injury has no relation to the offense, for someone wealthy might indeed allow himself to indulge

---

[52] Kant, *The Metaphysics of Morals*, 107 [6:334].
[53] Kant, *Lectures on Ethics*, 147 [27:373].

in a verbal insult on some occasion; yet the outrage he has done to someone's love or honor can still be quite similar to the hurt done to his pride if he is constrained by judgment and right not only to apologize publically to the one he has insulted but also to kiss his hand ..."[54] It is not the suffering that is important, but the fact that order, that is a moral order, is restored. Without justice there is no value in human life. Without our dignity as moral agents, without our self- and social-respect, our lives are without worth.

Kant commands: "*Be an honorable human being ... Rightful honor* ... consists in asserting one's worth as a human being in relation to others, as duty expressed by the saying, 'Do not make yourself a mere means for others but be at the same time an end for them.'"[55] Thus rightful or true honor is the manifestation of one's worth as a moral agent. Society reflects the praiseworthiness of the moral, upright life, by publicly affirming the value of honor and shaming those who act dishonorably by punishing them. A law abiding citizen, one who acts in accordance with strict duties of right is manifesting overtly his worth as a moral agent. "The motivating ground must be, not honour, but worthiness of honour."[56] Honor is not simply about arbitrary social esteem, it is, when rightful, a reflection of one's genuine moral worth.[57] We live well, that is, morally and honorably, not because we seek happiness or *eudaimonia*, but because so long as we live we will do so uprightly. "[An upright man] lives only from duty, not because he has the least taste for living."[58]

Ius talionis is more than just a mechanism of punishment, it is the reinforcement of a moral order via social practices rooted in the values of dignity and respect. These practices are the phenomenal face of a noumenal demand that we as moral agents interact as moral

---

[54] Kant, *The Metaphysics of Morals*, 106 [6:332].

[55] Ibid, 29 [6:236].

[56] Kant, *Lectures on Ethics*, 247 [29:632].

[57] In fact, as Kuehn notes, Kant is quite critical of Cicero's account of honor. See Manfred Kuehn, *Kant: A Biography*, 280.

[58] Kant, *Critique of Practical Reason*, 75 [5:88].

agents according to the moral law, respectful of freedom and so in accord with a doctrine of right. Thus, the following seemingly hyperbolic statement is put into proper context: "For if justice goes, there is no longer any value in human beings' living on the earth."[59]

CONCLUSION

If one gets to the root of Kant's practical philosophy, one finds in it a response to the seeming meaninglessness of human existence. Humanity has the role of doing nothing less than redeeming all of creation, and it does so by living morally. "Without man ... the whole of creation would be a mere wilderness, a thing in vain, and have no final end ... a good will is that whereby man's existence can alone possess an absolute worth, and in relation to which the existence of the world can have a *final end*."[60] Without justice there is no value in this world, for when justice goes it indicates that morality and with it dignity has gone as well. Woe upon us indeed that veer from the only source of absolute, inherent value of which the world is capable. That road to *eudaimonia*, pleasure, or consequentialism leads to degradation insofar as it implies everything has a price, everything is for sale. Respect is the fundamental human relation that must be promoted and adhered to if our lives, our society, and the world as a whole is to have any worth beyond a mere price.

Right, as indicated above, is not only the recognition of one's status as a dignified being demanding respect but its instantiation via the law. As Kant notes with respect to the moral law, "This law is to furnish the sensible world ... with the form of a world of the understanding." [61] We impose on the sensible world a moral order and thus make the phenomenal world approximate the noumenal by instantiating a moral order in nature. This is how value enters the world and it only remains so long as we do our part in maintaining

---

[59] Kant, *The Metaphysics of Morals*, 105 [6:332].
[60] Kant, "Part Two: Critique of Teleological Judgement," in *Critique of Judgement*, 108, 109.
[61] Kant, *Critique of Practical Reason*, 38 [5:43].

it. How else can a moral order come to be, unless we believe in it and act as though it were real?

Punishment is part and parcel to this moral worldview, included within a system of right guided by principles of respect and recognition. This practice serves both to reinforce and promulgate respect between persons as citizens. Criminals who affront our dignity must be punished if our value or dignity is to have any real existence. It must be recognized in order for it to be actual. Punishment thus symbolically recognizes the inherent value of both the criminal and the victim through institutionalized social practices meant to reinforce the worth of persons. The state is thus the guarantor of the meaningfulness of human existence insofar as it secures our worth and maintains respectful relations between people. Just as God maintains a moral and just order in the afterlife in the kingdom of ends by securing the highest good so the state operates as heaven on earth rewarding the good via rightful honor and punishing the bad in proportion to their wickedness.

MENCIUS: PLATO WITH A COUNTRY ON HIS SIDE. LOOKING TO CHINA FOR HELP WITH JURISPRUDENTIAL PROBLEMS

Seth Gurgel

Harmony is the baseline belief that threads most utopian theories of political science and jurisprudence, yet its many manifestations (including China's recent "harmonious society" program) have consistently been decried in the West as an enemy of individualism. E. H. Carr perhaps said it best when he declared that self-interested, egoistic realism has proven ascendant over every idealistic political and philosophical theory, yet it suffers from one fatal flaw—it is unfulfilling:

> [Humans] will continue to seek escape from the logical consequences of realism in the vision of an international order which, as soon as it crystallizes itself into concrete political form, becomes tainted with self-interest and hypocrisy, and once more be attacked with the instruments of realism.[1]

Carr's basic contention (contested of course) is that realism's strength lies in its powerful critique that human self-interest will stand in the way of any utopian success. He is also self-aware enough to recognize that the idea that humans are purely self-interested has never proven particularly satisfying: new types of idealism seem to crop up generation after generation, each eventually "disproved" by that same powerful, but unsatisfactory tool: liberal individualism. A similar problem exists in contemporary jurisprudence.

Jurisprudes will seemingly never be content with the idea that an unjust law can still be declared a law. Yet, theories that advocate inherent principles of justice rooted in natural law principles are often dismissed out of hand. Those theories that attempt to avoid natural law pitfalls and advocate for justice principles discovered in a deontological or other manner (i.e. a Dworkinian plumbing of the values

---

[1] E. H. Carr, *The Twenty Years' Crisis* (1939).

buried in our legal tradition) are attacked for allowing too much discretion to what will no doubt be self-interested judges applying their own brand of morality. We end up with unsatisfying, compromised, statements such as this one by R. P. Peerenboom: "Theories of natural law and natural rights ... may indeed be 'nonsense on stilts,' ... yet, if nonsense, they are very valuable nonsense, if myths, life-saving myths."[2] Of course, Bentham would be quick to note the converse of this statement has also proven true: How many times have lives been taken or rights been denied *on the very grounds* that natural rights or law denied those rights?

With that seeming dialectic evident in political and jurisprudential thought, it is little wonder that it also exists in concrete form in Western political and legal institutions. Perhaps the best example of the "undemocratic" in nearly all modern democracies is the increasing power of discretionary and relatively unaccountable administrative agencies. F. H. Hayek, in documenting the rise of administrative agencies, lamented the downfall of the rule of law as we understood it.[3] And yet, Max Weber declared bureaucratization an inevitable consequence of the post-industrial division of labor and the specialization of knowledge—how else are democratic societies to cope with this specialization but to place increasingly large amounts of discretionary power in the hands of technocrats capable of efficiently completing these complex tasks?[4] The fact that the American legal system has not yet determined how to classify the Administrative State within the United States' procrustean, tripartite division of the legislative, executive, and judicial branches has not in any way stopped its ascendancy. It persists even in spite of questions about its constitutionality and democratic nature.

Communitarian impulses are also threatening the hegemony of individualism in jurisprudential thought and international law, for

---

[2] R. P. Peerenboom, *Law and Morality in Ancient China : The Silk Manuscripts of Huang-Lao*, (Albany: State University of New York Press, 1993), 56.

[3] F. H. Hayek, *A Constitution of Liberty* (1960).

[4] Max Weber, *Economy and Society: On Bureaucracy.*

good or ill. International law's dirty little secret is that much of the progress made in the international human rights context is often made by the most undemocratic of means.[5] Jurisprudence seems unhappy with its Anglo-American roots. Dworkin, in his argument for "integrity" as a new political virtue, decries traditional liberal social contract thinking as an unsatisfactory model of social organization: "People can act almost as selfishly as people in a community of circumstances can. Each one can use the standing political machinery to advance his own interests or ideals."[6] Pure self-interest is at odds with the "fraternity" Dworkin finds appealing in the French democratic model.

This laundry list of dialectics is in no way exhaustive or comprehensive; it is merely intended to establish that the philosophy of law and politics is rife with cognitive dissonance, mainly when it tries to deal with the problems individualism presents when faced with the mounting demands of modern, pluralistic society. We need harmony and community, but where can we find it? This dissonance may be one reason why our culture still reveres and runs back to *The Republic,* even though a large part of it is dedicated to presenting an ideal society diametrically opposed to much of what contemporary Westerners hold dear: individualist notions of rights, democracy, even free markets.

PLATO, THE REPUBLIC, AND CHINESE PHILOSOPHY

The Republic, one of the seminal works of Western philosophy, is Plato's best known work. In it, Plato (re)creates a dialogue between Socrates and a cadre of Greek "interlocutors." Written in the form of a play, Socrates and his interlocutors examine the question of what Justice truly is, and whether the just man or the unjust man is ultimately more content in society. Unable to answer the question of what Justice would mean for an individual, Socrates leads the

---

[5] Joseph Weiler, NYU Law Professor, International Law Course Lecture, Spring 2008.
[6] Ronald Dworkin, *Law's Empire* (1986).

cast of characters through a philosophical exercise where they try to determine first what Justice would be on a state-level, believing that this exercise might be easier, and that it could then inform their quest to seek out what Justice would mean for the individual. The majority of the book is then dedicated to depicting this ideal society, which is, as mentioned above, noticeably devoid of many of the political institutions we (and Plato's contemporaries) hold essential to a rule of law society today.

One might argue that the society Plato advocates can be disregarded as a mere hypothetical that was really aimed at emphasizing individual justice, that it must be taught to give proper historical context to students of Western history, or that it is rich enough as philosophical text that one can ignore its long-since abrogated political theory and still gain an inordinate amount of other wisdom. Those are all plausible and valid reasons for teaching it. But it is also plausible that it is still read *precisely* because it presents an alluring, compelling vision of life that is fascinating in its foreignness. If this has merit, it presents a problem: how can it be that Plato's *Republic* remains one of the purest, best, and (seductively) most appealing notions of the ideal when it directly espouses a vision contrary to many of the most fundamental concepts of our domestic and international institutions?

One argument could be that the *Republic* is the primary Western source for explanations of the "undemocratic" phenomena listed above. Plato's "Guardians," those selected and bred to lead the people, are critical in understanding the constant pull evident throughout Western history (evident even in our Founding Fathers) for rule by the elites, and if not government by elites, than at least government by technocrats. The Philosopher King explains in part how popular presidents like Lincoln and Roosevelt could be rather cavalier with critical tenets of the Constitution during their presidencies with little *post facto* criticism. It gives credence to Dostoyevsky's Grand Inquisitor, who chides Christ for not understanding that people will abandon free will in an instant for the promise of a strong leader who will fill their bellies. Finally, it is perhaps most helpful in presenting an interlocutor who reminds us that Jeremy Waldron is right to posit that we disagree most ardently about the things we hold dear: *The Republic* is an incredible phenomenon in our society—a widely-read and respected fundamental text that ostensibly espouses an ideal society quite different from our liberal, egalitarian ideal.

This does not mean that we could or would seek to implement *The Republic's* political system, but there should be no question that it is an essential part of the conversation. But if Plato and Aristotle, Dostoyevsky and Bentham, Dworkin and Hart can be part of the debate, indeed, *must* be part of the debate, why not Chinese thought?

I believe half of it is an honest lack of knowledge (or access) to Chinese thought, which will surely be solved as the world gradually flattens. I hope that the other half is not simple disrespect. If one is to read ancient Chinese political thought alongside the careful building of Plato's ideal society, the similarities are striking. More than that, Chinese history represents the best (if still quite imperfect) attempt at manifesting *The Republic*'s society. Indeed, two thousand years of political and legal thought were dedicated to perfecting Mencius's government consisting of the best, by the best, but *for* the people. The Han dynasty built an empire that rivaled its contemporary Rome in power and sophistication, but it also created a competent, effective administrative state the likes of which did not exist in the West until Britain and France followed suit 1500 years later, when they finally felt Weber's call of historical necessity.[7] This did not happen in a philosophical vacuum: the choice was not simply between a tyrant and a democracy. The Chinese made a political decision espoused by one of the most revered Western philosophers without ever consulting him. Modern Western democracies are now evincing similar political decisions: the administrative state seems necessary in spite of its handling by technocrats armed

---

[7] Which leads to the question posed to me in conversation by Professor Frank Upham (April 2010), if it was "historical necessity for the West, what was it for the Han?"

with copious amounts of discretion and varying degrees of democratic legitimacy.

PLATO AND MENCIUS

There is much historical parallel between the two philosophers. Mencius (372-289 B.C.) lived the first twenty-three years of his life as a contemporary of Plato. After Confucius himself, he is considered the greatest and most influential advocate of Confucianism in Chinese history, and in many ways, he surpassed his predecessor.[8] Mencius lived during the Warring States period, which was marked by both a fierce, violent contest for power between several rival states, and a concomitant robust flowering of political and moral thought that sought to bring peace.

War was not necessarily Plato's primary concern; rather it was the internal unrest occurring in Athens the most worried him. The unraveling of Pericles' democracy had brought upheaval, manifesting itself in the execution of his mentor, Socrates. Plato sought to sound "a warning to all Athenians that without respect for law, leadership and a sound education for the young, their city would continue to decay. Plato wanted to rescue Athens from degeneration by reviving that sense of community that had at one time made the *polis* great."[9] There are certainly many salient differences between the philosophies of Plato and Mencius; but, there are also strong similarities between their images of the ideal society: they both developed comparable theories of virtue, predicated on the idea that man is innately good and that this potential can be developed through education.[10] While there are still strong differences between the two, I believe their metaphysical similarities

---

[8] Carson Chang, "The Significance of Mencius," *Philosophy East and West* 8.1-2 (1958), 37.

[9] Steven Kreis, "The History Guide" http://www.historyguide.org/ancient/lecture8b.html.

[10] Peerenboom, 121. Note that Peerenboom challenges the more widespread notion that Mencius is an innatist, and wants to claim that he was nearly as much a pragmatist as was Confucius.

allowed each to advocate a type of class-based meritocracy led by philosopher-kings.

If Plato and Mencius were both indeed alerting their societies about the need for respect for reason and for a division of labor based on merit, Mencius must be regarded as more successful in this regard. He adopted Confucius's teachings, refining the relatively ambiguous key virtues of Confucianism and clarifying their meaning. Moreover, it was Mencius who solidified Confucian ideals of government and politics by connecting them strongly to the Confucian values of filial piety and anchoring them deep in Chinese myth and legend.[11] The political conception of the emperor as both the most filial son as well as the father worthy of every citizen's piety would prove to have great staying power, serving as the basis for the structure of government and education in dynasties as late as the Song (960-1279) and Ming (1368-1644).

The Concept of Virtue

While this is not a paper contrasting Plato and Mencius's theories of the ultimate good, it is important that one have at least a rudimentary knowledge of Mencius's conception of virtue. Mencius was the first Confucian to espouse a system of virtue based on the doctrine of ideas, adopting a teleological approach much different than his forebears and very similar to that of Plato.[12] Plato and Mencius both intimated that the pursuit of the good was the highest ideal and that it had been ordained outside of the physical world, even if they may have differed on which virtues constitute that good.[13] Mencius outlines his four virtues below.

---

[11] Carson Chang, "The Significance of Mencius," *Philosophy East and West* 8.1-2 (1958), 37.

[12] *Ibid.* at 39.

[13] *Ibid.* at 41; Indeed, Plato rarely talked of a transcendent good or overriding truth, but rather was content to intimate it. Plato's four cardinal virtues are Wisdom, Courage, Moderation, and Justice. Note that there is considerable discussion about the degree to which Mencius depended on a universal theory of forms or class concepts like Plato. For our purposes, it is enough that he is not a strict pragmatist.

> As far as natural tendencies are concerned, it is possible for one to do good; this is what I mean by being good. If one does what is not good, that is not the fault of one's capacities. The mind of pity and commiseration is possessed by all human beings [rén]; the mind of shame and aversion is possessed by all human beings [rightness]; the mind of respectfulness and reverence is possessed by all human beings [decorum]; and the mind that knows right and wrong is possessed by all human beings [wisdom] ... rén, rightness, decorum and wisdom are not infused into us from without. We definitely possess them ... Therefore it is said, 'Seek and you will get it; let go and you will lose it.' That some differ from others by as much as twice or five times, or an incalculable order of magnitude, it is because there those who are unable to fully develop their capacities.[14]

Whether Plato's "justice" or Mencius's "*rén,*" both were seen as ideals that were attainable by human beings, at least by those who both were talented and steadfast in their pursuit of them.

MENCIUS'S HISTORICAL ADVANTAGE[15]

One critical factor in Mencius's success in having his message adopted wholesale was that he had an appeal to history that Plato did not. Both philosophers used inductive reasoning in order to prove their concept of the good. But throughout the *Republic*, Plato is often forced to reason from his own analogies or hypotheticals (such

---

[14] Mencius, quoted in William Theodore de Bary & Irene Bloom, *Sources of Chinese Tradition: From Earliest Times to 1600*, 149 (Columbia University Press, 1999). Note on Ren: Mencius's 仁 (rén) has been interpreted in a variety of ways: humaneness, benevolence, mercy, and the above-mentioned "pity and commiseration." All of these are denotations of the word which fall far short of its actual depth: it is the axial virtue of the four and is therefore as hopelessly indefinable as Plato's "justice," especially when one attempts to translate it into English using concepts that we may find far less problematic. I will therefore simply use the term rén in order to obviate the reader's appropriating an unproblematic reading of the word.

[15] I recognize that there are many political and historical explanations for why Plato and Mencius's ideas were or were not adopted by their respective governments. This article cannot address those theories, rather it attempts to analyze the theoretical and rhetorical differences that made each more or less likely to be adopted.

as the Cave or the Ship Captain[16]) to reinforce his hermeneutic. Indeed the Republic itself had to first be imagined in order to prove what justice would mean for the individual. Mencius had a far more effective tool that made his statements almost "empirical": the ancient kingdoms of the "sage emperors" Yao and Shun, China's kings David and Solomon.

The first chapters of a seminal text of the Chinese civilization, the *Shujing* (Classic of History), contain the *Canon of Yao* and the *Canon of Shun*, claimed to be the events and pronouncements of these two sage rulers who purportedly ruled around 2200 B.C.[17] Yao was the ideal ruler, who personified civic and family virtue. His "[virtue] radiated out in successive degrees of kinship, so that all humankind was harmonized in one loving family."[18] Here, eighteen hundred years before Mencius, we have a foundational myth emphasizing both community and rule by the virtuous. In choosing his successor, Shun—a low-ranking official of quite poor parentage but who was considered to be the most virtuous in the kingdom— to ascend the throne after him rather than his own son, Yao established a standard that promoted both the virtue he embodied and preference for rule by merit (in being virtuous) above primogeniture and family connections. De Bary and Bloom point out in their *Sources of Chinese Tradition* that, while like most foundational texts, the *Canons*' accuracy might be questioned, the key is "how these texts were appropriated within mainstream Chinese culture… it is true of almost any major tradition that its foundational texts exhibit a powerful mythic quality and, regardless of their exact provenance or historicity, prove no less formative of tradition and axial to a civilization for partaking of this trans-historical, mythic quality."[19]

As the later sections will prove, Mencius fully exploited that already two-thousand-year-old parable to corroborate his theories via

---

[16] *The Republic,* Book VI
[17] De Bary and Bloom. 29.
[18] De Bary and Bloom, 24.
[19] De Bary and Bloom, 23.

means that border on the theological. Indeed, one might claim that in a Dworkinian sense, the dominance of Mencius's theory over the other competing philosophies of the day was predicated on his successful harmonization of the seminal texts of the (already ancient) Chinese culture with the Confucian world view. This is most obvious when one reads his opinions on rule by the virtuous elite.

The Sage King

> From the compass and square comes the ultimate standard for circles and squares, and from the sage comes the ultimate standard in human relations ... *all that is necessary is to take Yao and Shun as the model* ... There are just two ways: having *rén* and not having *rén*. One whose oppression of his people is extreme will himself be killed and his state will be lost.[20] (emphasis added)

> Confucius said, "Great indeed was Yao as a ruler. Only Heaven is great, and yet Yao patterned himself after Heaven. How vast, how magnificent! The people could find no name for it. What a ruler was Shun! How lofty, how majestic! He possessed the empire as if it were nothing to him." *As Yao and Shun ruled the empire, it could not have been done without fully devoting their minds to it, but they did not devote themselves to tilling the fields.*[21] (emphasis added)

In Book V of *The Republic*, Socrates is asked what ails the Athenian state. Socrates believes it is simple: states have the wrong rulers, whose skill lies not in pursuing virtue but in speaking "with the loudest mob."[22] Plato was one of the few Athenian intelligentsia unconvinced that democracy was the most elevated form of government, and was convinced that group decisions made by political

---

[20] *Ibid.*, at 137.
[21] *Ibid.* at 134.
[22] In real life, Plato was part of a losing faction that was opposed to the Athenian democracy, and presumably believed that one of their number was more fitted to rule than those democratically elected. So this part of the dialogue may have been more personal than most.

dilettantes could never be more effective than those made by the most competent leader. Socrates then continued his attack on Athenian democracy with a broader claim, that intra-state conflicts will continue and justice will never manifest itself until philosophers are made rulers or until present rulers and kings show themselves to be philosophers.[23] This is where the concept of the Philosopher King is born. Having now established the character of the true philosopher, in Book VI Socrates sets himself to the task of showing why the philosopher would, in the ideal state, be the best ruler. Benjamin Jowett sums up Plato's Philosopher King this way:

> In language which seems to reach beyond the horizon of that age and country, he is described as "the spectator of all time and all existence." He has the noblest gifts of nature, and makes the highest use of them. All his desires are absorbed in the love of wisdom, which is the love of truth. None of the graces of a beautiful soul are wanting in him; neither can he fear death, or think much of human life. It is he who understands truly the nature of reality.[24]

Mencius's four virtues do not conflict with this Platonic answer to the philosopher-king's qualifications to rule, but this description, which relies heavily on the concept of wisdom, does not encapsulate what is most important for Mencius: that the ruler be moral. Wisdom (as well as *ren,* rightness, and decorum) were means to a more important end: to cultivate the moral dispositions, critical to the virtuous ruling of the sage-king.[25] In fact, where Plato was often hesitant to speak of "the good" even if it may have been implied in his work, Mencius made it clear that rigorous adoption of his four virtues was to be undertaken precisely for the sake of attaining the good.[26] Mencius seemed to appropriate the stories of Yao, Shun and

---

[23] Note that later in this paper, a Song dynasty neo-Confucian reformer makes almost the same argument about how the rule of law stunts the pursuit of real justice. See note 52.

[24] Benjamin Jowett, *The Republic, Introduction and Analysis,* Book VI. Available at http://tinyurl.com/3tgk3c9.

[25] Peerenboom 122.

[26] Chang at 41; See also Jowett at Book VI.

other sage kings of the past in a nearly theological manner, "Mencius's discussion of the matters of state draw on historical memory ... He seems to reclaim, in memory, the moral aura of a time before the beginning of the dynastic system ..."[27] I would propose that it is precisely this character of Mencius' Confucianism that made it so comprehensive, it possessed aspects of both idealist and pragmatic philosophy which were theologically harmonized with the universalizing and mythical aspects of ancient Chinese history and legend.

Mencius the Theologian?

Mencius effectively incorporated the symbols and myths of his time period into a political philosophy that could not just be discussed, but could also be *believed*. The theologian Paul Tillich famously remarked that "The task of the philosopher primarily involves developing the questions, whereas the task of the theologian primarily involves developing the answers to these questions." However, it should be remembered that the two tasks overlap and include one another: the theologian must be somewhat of a philosopher and vice versa, for Tillich's notion of faith as "ultimate concern" necessitates that the "theological answer be correlated with, compatible with, and in response to the general ontological question which must be developed independently from the answers." According to this definition, Mencius proves to be more theologian than philosopher: he was seeking answers to the problem of a disharmonious society.

Tillich also talks about how one constructs a belief system:

> Ultimate reality transcends any attempt to describe it adequately, and can only be described by the use of symbols. The language of faith is a symbolic language used to describe ultimate reality. For example, the word 'God' is a symbol for ultimate reality. Therefore, to argue about whether God exists or does not exist is futile and meaningless. . . . [M]yths are symbols of faith, which tell stories to portray situations

---

[27] De Bary and Bloom, 115. For more discussion of the use of symbols and myth in theology see Paul Tillich, *Dynamics of Faith* (New York :Harper and Row, 1957).

> of ultimate concern. Myths may be 'broken' or 'unbroken.' Unbroken myths are myths which are accepted as literal statements of reality. Broken myths are myths which are interpreted as myths, as symbolic statements of reality.[28]

By any standard, Mencius was more successful at anchoring his philosophy into the myths of ancient China, whether "broken" or "unbroken. Foremost among these are the myths of Yao and Shun. Indeed, moving from the theological to the jurisprudential (if they're really that far apart), one can witness the Dworkinian dominance Mencius's theory exerted over other competing philosophies of the day in his successful harmonization of the classics of Chinese culture with the Confucian worldview.

> From the compass and square comes the ultimate standard for circles and squares, and from the sage comes the ultimate standard in human relations…*all that is necessary is to take Yao and Shun as the model*…There are just two ways: having *rén* and not having *rén*. One whose oppression of his people is extreme will himself be killed and his state will be lost.[29]

Plato had a similar king, the philosopher king. As mentioned above, this king had "the noblest gifts of nature...the love of truth. None of the graces of a beautiful soul were wanting in him... He understood the true nature of reality." There was only one problem, Mencius was telling people who they were and to whom they should aspire from stories they already treasured as their own. Plato was telling them what their messy democratic society was most decidedly not and was calling them to turn from their evil ways. He had no Yao and no Shun— the man who had taught him a majority of what he had learned had been executed by his countrymen.

The Argument for Exclusiveness

To both Platonists and Confucians, being the expert on virtue

---

[28] Paul Tillich, *Dynamics of Faith* (New York: Harper & Row, 1957), 46, 50
[29] De Bary and Bloom, 137.

meant the right to "impose" that virtue on the rest of the population: like Plato, the Confucian scholars that upheld Mencius's beliefs had little problem with censorship and the repression of other ideas. In Book Two, Plato drew a distinction between stories that were morally uplifting and those that were not. Censors of literature were to be appointed by the leaders of the state to ensure that only "good" stories are taught to the children. Plato held a disdain for poets, artists, and other "false teachers" who used their rhetorical and creative skills to sow disharmony and lack of respect for the four virtues. This exclusivist idea—reminiscent more of religion than of the philosophical tradition—of the censorship of the arts is continued in Book III.

In China, the twin pillars of support Mencius maintained for Confucianism proved to be even stronger arguments for censorship: first, his idealist strain similar to Plato's Forms necessitated that virtue could be understood, and if understood, it could also be misunderstood.[30] In other words, he seems to be far more on the "answers side" of Tillich's spectrum than the "questions side." According to Mencius, Variations of the "Way" (道 *dao*) that advocated for a style of governance counter to the way of Yao and Shun should not be permitted as they would prove morally damaging.

Second, since Confucianism typically took a pragmatic rather than idealist form, a Confucian minister would argue that even if the ultimate truth of a particular theory were in doubt, the mere presence of conflicting theories was certain to bring unrest and disharmony. Minister Dong Zhongshu made just this argument to King Wu early in the Han dynasty:

> The teachers of today have different doctrines, and men expound diverse theories; the various schools of philosophy differ in their ways, and their principles do not agree. Thus

---

[30] It should be noted that Plato was making a case for censorship in what is described by many historians as one of the most tolerant societies in the ancient world. Of course, Plato may have doubted the true tolerance of the Athenians who eventually put his teacher and mentor Socrates to death for corrupting the young. Hendrik Willem Van Loon, *Tolerance*, (New York: Boni and Liveright, 1925), 35.

> the ruler has no means by which to achieve unity, the laws and institutions undergo frequent changes, and the people do not know what to honor. Your unworthy servant considers that whatever is not encompassed by the Six Disciplines and the arts of Confucius should be suppressed and not allowed to continue further, and evil and vain theories be stamped out. Only then will unity be achieved, the laws be made clear, and the people know what to follow.[31]

Emperor Wu acceded to the suggestion, and Confucianism became the official teaching of the dynasty, assuming its place as the predominant governmental philosophy for the next two thousand years.[32] To some, Wu's action and Dong's encouragement to do so may simply be plain censorship, indistinguishable from censorship practiced by dictators throughout history (it certainly does to most of us imbued from birth with democratic sensibilities). Of course, Wu most likely based his decision on a self-interested desire for the perpetuation of his family's reign as many other totalitarian regimes have rather than a nuanced examination of the various metaphysical pros and cons of the then-competing philosophies. That was of no matter; he could leave that to the bureaucracy (discussed below).

Theological Rites

Once Confucianism became part of the regime, its pragmatic, rites-aspect allowed for universal participation in the search for societal harmony. The idea that abstract concepts be relayed via age and

---

[31] De Bary and Bloom, 311. While beyond the scope of this article, the author would be remiss not to point out the resonance this passage shares with the Chinese Communist Party's recent emphasis on building a "harmonious society and that society's implications."

[32] It should be noted that Wu's reign was not remotely close to the Confucian ideal, nor did it do away with competing ideologies, which persisted. Indeed, Legalism (a philosophy that advocated a Machiavellian type of rule of law) persisted down to 50 B.C, and other theories were to exert considerable influence on future dynasties, Buddhist thought during the Tang being the most well-known. The key here is that Dong's style of reasoning was the type of reasoning that would be alluded to each time Confucianism's influence faded throughout the centuries: the combination of the idealism inherited from Mencius and the utterly pragmatic basis of the theory in family relationships was a formidable rhetorical wall to overcome.

intelligence-appropriate means gels very well with Plato's conception regarding the simpler minds of children. Plato acknowledged that many of the arts exhibited both *figurative* and *literal* meanings, but he argued that young children could not always make distinctions between things literal and figurative.[33] The establishment of rites served this purpose in China, similar to their more prominent role in religion: rites allow for meaning to grow as one's own ideas mature. The rite of performing the rosary retains its meaning even as one becomes conscious of its more important figurative meanings. Confucian rites maintained a similar genius in their simplicity: first, obey your parents. Next, obey the rites, which established a simple, understandable matrix of who is to give respect and who is to be respected in nearly every social situation.

Unsurprisingly, the patron saint of the filial son was Shun, the second philosopher king. When Yao asked about him, his ministers responded that "His father is stupid, his mother is deceitful, his half brother Xiang is arrogant. Yet he has been able to live in harmony with them and to be splendidly filial. He has controlled himself and not come to wickedness."[34]

It is small wonder that the complex relationship between virtue and filial piety, between king and commoner, between the ideal of harmony and the practicality of simple rites in which everyone can participate produced a (1) community bond in China unlike few other places in the world, (2) a respect for a meritocracy that was presumed talented and virtuous (but respected regardless, just as children love parents who are anything but ideal), and finally, (3) a morally-based resilience among the people to endure harsh regimes while maintaining hope for the best. China had the infrastructure, philosophy and rhetoric of *The Republic* in place. This ideology lends naturally to concept of a rule by the elites: men and women were to conduct themselves first according to the role in which they

---

[33] Benjamin Jowett, *The Republic*, *Introduction and Analysis* Books II and III. http://tinyurl.com/3tgk3c9

[34] De Bary and Bloom, 30.

had be placed, to cultivate virtue in response to that role, those who were most successful and most worthy in doing so would be selected by those above them to be the future leaders of the country.

But were their hopes for a philosopher king fulfilled at a greater rate than in other countries? Did a philosopher king ever rule, or at least come to power at a higher degree of regularity than elsewhere? Or rather, did the myth of Yao and Shun merely perpetuate thousands of years of relatively unchallenged kingly rule, no different than the history of autocracy in any other nation, no more laudable than the divine right of kings and perhaps even more tyrannical because any ruler would face a filial, docile public?[35]

Just as in medieval European thought, Chinese kings had the mandate of heaven.[36] Rather than pushing low-level officials like Shun to the top based on their virtue, China still practiced dynastic succession which was as unpredictable as it was in other countries around the world. The real power of China's posture as a *Republic*-type country was more contingent on the fact that the people of China were better conditioned than those in other countries *to accept* a philosopher king than that there were disproportionate numbers of sages ascending the throne. As Plato predicted, this communitarian predisposition allowed for great periods of prosperity when a virtuous emperor ruled, but perhaps allowed for immoral hegemons to wreak even more damage on the population than one would on a population less inclined to treat the sovereign as their father. But if the monarchs of pre renaissance China and Europe were relatively similar, the ruling classes directly beneath those monarchs were drastically different.

---

[35] It has been noted that Mencius wrote that revolution was a natural result of kings not fulfilling their duties. It is quite possible that this was more a warning to kings than an instruction to the people. This question cuts across a lot of Confucian thought; scholars are divided on how individuals were to deal with divided loyalty between family and government. For example, if one's father had committed a crime, should he be reported? Most cases seems to have been dealt with in quite a simple manner—punish both: the father for the crime and the son for his lack of filial piety.

[36] De Bary and Bloom, 144.

THE MERITOCRACY

> Without noblemen, there would be no one to rule the country people, and without the country people there would be no one to feed the noblemen ... Some labor with their minds, others labor with their strength. Those who labor with their minds govern others, while those who labor with their strength are governed by others. Those who are governed by others support them; those who govern others are supported by them.[37]

> Those who keep to the Mean nurture those who do not; those who have talent nurture those who have not. Therefore people take pleasure in having exemplary fathers and elder brothers. If those who keep to the Mean were to cast aside those who do not, and if those who have talent were to cast aside those who have not, the space between the exemplary and those found wanting would narrow to less than an inch.[38]

The mitochondria that drove the Chinese search for the ideal was the meritocracy. Daniel Bell mentions in his book *East Meets West* that a far greater reverence for the educated exists in China than in the United States, and that it is a legacy, in part, of the ancient Chinese civil service examinations and the massive, sophisticated bureaucracy that the examinations filled.[39] The development of a merit-based bureaucracy peopled by the brightest of the country regardless of class fifteen hundred years before it was conceived of in Europe should be regarded as a political invention of China every bit as momentous as paper, the printing press, or gun powder. It is in training hundreds of thousands of the best and brightest of the kingdom in Confucian thought and empowering them to rule, that the Chinese came as close to establishing a class of Platonic Guardians as any culture ever did.

---

[37] De Bary and Bloom, 132.
[38] De Bary and Bloom, 141.
[39] Daniel Bell, *East Meets West: Human Rights and Democracy in East Asia* (Princeton University Press, 2000), 130.

The sheer scope of the Chinese bureaucratic enterprise is staggering, especially when one considers that at the same time the Roman republic had no established bureaucracy. Already by the end of the first century B.C. (one hundred years after China had been unified), there were some three thousand students enrolled at the "Great Academy" established to fill the Han bureaucracy; in the latter Han that number grew to more than thirty thousand students studying in, by then, the all-Confucian Academy.[40] At the same time, provincial schools were established and the Confucian tradition of education was spread across China.[41] The curriculum at the Great Academy was composed of the Confucian Five Classics, the basis of Chinese education that was not revamped until the Qing dynasty (1644-1912).[42]

Learning at these schools was mostly by rote. Consistent with Dong Zhongshu's advice to Emperor Wu it was dedicated to the "creation of bureaucratic generalists familiar with an accepted ethical outlook and body of knowledge, not with the growth of knowledge or with academic specialization."[43] (It should be noted though, that in their examinations, the students were required to think critically about modern political problems, and were to use their knowledge of the classics to fashion solutions to those problems.)

While many might critique this pedagogy, even this, too, seems quite consistent with Plato's earlier remarks about censorship of the bad or immoral. The goal of his system of training and education for the Guardians was to preserve the unity of the ideal state. In Book V, Socrates has to answer the complaint that his communitarian policies would in fact de-personalize almost every aspect of state life.[44] He responds that that is exactly right; personal ambitions, greed, and

---

[40] Bloom, 312; it should be noted that the original founding of the bureaucracy in the Qin and early Han was a combination of Legalist and Confucian thought. It was not until the later Han and thereafter that it was completely dominated by Confucianism.

[41] California State University of Pomona Asian Studies Department *Overview of the Chinese Bureaucracy.* http://www.csupomona.edu/~plin/ls201/confucian2.html

[42] *Ibid.*

[43] *Ibid.*

[44] *The Republic,* Book VI

petty personal jealousies are the very things that disrupt the state. They breed animosities among and between people. Socrates wants unity and harmony in the state, at whatever cost.[45] In that sense, the education at the Great Academy was in concord with the training of the Guardians.

But the scholar-officials were to be more than ruling automatons; they were also to be China's literati and artists for the two thousand years of Chinese dynastic rule. Politically, skill in art and especially poetry (all written within the parameters of the Confucian ideal, of course) influenced one's accomplishment in court life.[46] The Emperor and his courtiers were all supposed to be accomplished poets, and every official ceremony or banquet would be celebrated in verse. This is completely in line with Plato's ideal for artists:

> Let our artists rather be those who are gifted to discern the true nature of the beautiful and graceful; then will our youth dwell in a land of health, amid fair sights and sounds, and receive the good in everything; and beauty, the effluence of fair works, shall flow into the eye and ear, like a health-giving breeze from a purer region, and insensibly draw the soul from earliest years into likeness and sympathy with the beauty of reason.[47]

In China this meant that the poet-scholar was in the center of a social network in which his art was public and conventional. Sharing a similar education with other scholar-officials, he could make allusions to the classics which they would all readily recognize; he wrote in a style to which they all conformed. This meant that art also pursued a Confucian ideal, rather than what many Westerners might conceive art to manifest, a strong expression of individualism and often subversion. Masterful levels of skill and detail were developed within these rigid constraints.[48] This may have been

---

[45] *The Republic*, Book III
[46] De Bary and Bloom.
[47] *The Republic,* Book III
[48] Columbia University, East Asian Curriculum Project. http://afe.easia.columbia.edu/china/lit/scholar.htm

misery for the Western rugged-individualist artist, but is entirely consistent of Plato's view of art and artists, and again, meant that China's autocracy was something different from a bare tyranny, as the ruling classes comprised a large number of those who "pursued the good."

An entire cadre of students schooled in exactly the same thought would also solve a rule of law problem for a idealist state like Plato's that was supposed to have few rules and subjective, "pragmatic" rule-making. Earlier in *The Republic*, Plato attacks the idea of a society governed by myriad, overly detailed laws. He argues that the ideal ruler should individualize law for each specific person and situation, just as a doctor would individualize care for a patient.[49] The goal of laws for Plato is to fashion just laws that create just citizens. It was the same for a Confucian scholar—generalized laws would prove both over and under inclusive. They would create people who avoided punishment rather than sought virtue: a lowest-common denominator type of society that had abandoned the search for the good. Of course one of the basic problems with adopting a system based on the "rule of men" (人制 *ren zhi*) rather than on a rule of law (法制 *fa zhi*) is that it often sacrifices predictability and equality for individualization, which could then lead to favoritism, partiality, and discrimination. A strict, standardized curriculum that stresses rote learning of a single branch of thought over individualized thought obviates some of this concern.

First, citizens need not worry as much about equal application of the law if students are drilled in the school of thought, spanning both the practical as well as core metaphysical beliefs; second, the law's "predictability" might even be increased for the average individual: there would be no specialized knowledge of the law required of a common citizen, rather the question would simply be whether they conformed with the requirements of virtue in any particular case. Law was taken from the courtroom to the confessional.

There are obvious critiques of this from a rule of law perspec-

[49] *The Republic* Book IV.

tive, but for our purposes, it is worthwhile seeing how this would fulfill the Platonic ideal of individualized law. Every person would be judged according to the same standard— justice—but that would be a standard that would expect more from the scholar than the farmer.[50]

This debate was largely moot, for laws did accrue over time. The Confucian ideal of people guided and judged simply on their conformity with virtue was joined early on in the Han dynasty with Legalist notions that sought for clear rules and clear punishments.[51] However, the debate between rule of law or rule of men was resurrected often, as it is here by the Song Dynasty neo-Confucian scholar Chen Liang, who argues in a sophisticated manner against the rule of law's "selfish expediency" around the time of Aquinas:

> My own humble opinion is: the world must have laws, regulations, and institutions, but laws, regulations, and institutions can operate only when proper personnel are appointed. We have made many institutional regulations in order to be able to say to the world that, just on the remote chance that there were no proper personnel, our institutions could still function. What promotes such an attitude, however, is actually selfish [expediency], and this is the reason why corruption in the world is incessant and unending. If those who set up laws and regulations would adopt my viewpoint and change laws and regulations [to allow the bureaucrats more discretion] not only would the day come when we could cure the source of this corruption but also from this day forward the intent of the sages during the golden ages...in establishing laws and institutions... would become clearly manifest.[52]

Chen was intimating the debates between Dicey and K. C.

---

[50] Note that laws that did develop did indeed take account of rank, and they were not all skewed to favor the officials. While it was of course true that officials would be exempt from petty crimes, they were also held far more accountable for "sins of the flesh," as they were expected to have overcome those passions.

[51] Shen Bu Hai, Legalist Philosopher, University of Hong Kong Legalist Philosophers Web Resources, http://www.hku.hk/philodep/ch/Shen%20Bu%20Hai.htm

[52] De Bary and Bloom, 651.

Davis about the need for discretion in bureaucratic appointment and affairs.[53] He argued that contradictorily, the desire for a rule of law to constrain the discretion of bureaucrats, if taken too far, would actually encourage bureaucrats to break the law if they had to choose between following the law and doing what they knew to be the right action. In Chen's view, laws were necessary, but they would never trump having a virtuous leader, and the sages "never went so far as to say that institutions could function without proper personnel."[54]

But who is to say that the "proper personnel" would necessarily choose to work for the bureaucracy? Bell claims that this is where Mencius and Plato would differ, that Plato spoke of enlightened ones being "*burdened* by the task of public duty, [whereas] true enlightenment lay outside the cave" while Confucius claimed rather that it was his duty to serve the public, that a person "cultivates himself to ease the burden on the whole populace."[55] This idea was echoed by Mencius:

> After Tang sent messengers three times to entreat him he changed and with an altered countenance, said, "Were I allowed to remain amidst these fields I might delight in the way of Yao and Shun. But might it not be better if I caused this ruler to become a Yao or a Shun? Might it not

---

[53] Dicey, a nineteenth-century British jurist, was a strict procedural formalist who struck out strongly against the growing threat of administrative agencies in Great Britain. His first principle of Rule of Law is that "no person can be punished or made to suffer in body or goods" without law and due process. His point here is that administrative decisions that exact any type of "penalty" should be legislated first. K. C. Davis, also a procedural formalist, but a more moderate one, claims that Dicey's thoughts were ignorant of history and of the necessity for administrative agencies. Davis concluded that we are to fear punishment or suffering in body or goods only when administrative power is capricious. Furthermore, he stated that there are many times when administrative decisions are *necessary* (i.e. when *ex ante* information is unavailable). Finally, mirroring Chen, he stated that there are even times when administrative discretion is not just necessary, but also *desirable*, especially in decisions that required high "institutional competence" or detailed "substantive justice." For in those situations, administrative experts would be most likely to craft the just decision.

[54] De Bary and Bloom, 651.

[55] Bell, 287.

be better if I caused this people to become the people of Yao and Shun?[56]

Bell is correct in his assessment that both the philosophy and history of Confucian cultures established a belief that "government by the best" was both desirable and the duty of the Chinese intelligentsia. He supports this theory with examples from contemporary Japan and Singapore, where the top students from the key universities regularly go into public service rather than private life, and they are accordingly given more discretion than Western bureaucrats.[57] But I believe that he is too quick to assume that Plato would disagree with this.

There are two reasons for this. The first is that this reading of the Cave analogy seems to neglect Socrates' admonishment of Glaucon who claims just what Bell says, that the man who has made it out of the cave will not want to go back into the cave. Socrates points out that the goal of life is not happiness, but justice, and justice requires that one who has discovered wisdom *will* desire to go back.[58] Secondly, striking similarities between Plato and Mencius on the ideal of harmony are found in Book III where Plato espouses his virtue of temperance. Temperance for Plato is achieved by the individual when he quashes his lesser desires for the good of the more noble ones.[59] He extends the concept of temperance to the state by claiming that for a state to be temperate would mean for it to run harmoniously.[60] To do this, every class in the state has to cooperate with the other classes (like the passions inside a man must be harmonized within him); the classes would then recognize, agree with, and actively endorse the functions of all classes in the state.[61] Thus the state may be said to be master of itself, in that the three classes

---

[56] De Bary and Bloom.
[57] Bell, 288
[58] *The Republic* Book VII
[59] This is completely consistent with Mencius who differentiates between the gentleman and the "little man" who follows his desires.
[60] *The Republic* Book III
[61] *Ibid.*

will function smoothly as a whole: "Harmony is diffused through the whole, making the dwellers in the city to be of one mind, and attuning the upper and middle and lower classes like the strings of an instrument, whether you suppose them to differ in wisdom, strength or wealth."[62]

Harmony for Plato meant knowing which class you belonged to and then knowing your role. The role for the Guardians was to rule. It is striking how similar this is to Mencius's view. The rites would teach one to respect those in a higher position than one was, but even more than that, the lesson in those rites was that one should know oneself and one's limitations and defer to those who were more capable, just as Yao passed over his own son to place Shun in power.[63] So, contrary to Bell, it was not that Plato did not espouse the virtue of the best and brightest choosing to work for the state, but rather, that it did not catch on the way Mencius and Confucius's conception of rule by the best did.

CONCLUSION

Jeremy Waldron, in putting forward his robust theory of the role of the legislature in a rule of law democracy, grounds his premise on the fact that we are a society that is inherently postured to disagree with one another, not just about simple matters of policy, but also in our most basic beliefs. I believe he is correct. As mentioned in the forward, the legal community currently faces a number of philosophical challenges. One has to deal with the recognition that considerable amounts of discretion are exercised within our democratic system absent true accountability. How can we ground this burgeoning regulatory state in some sort of democratic account-

---

[62] Benjamin Jowett, *The Republic, Introduction and Analysis,* Book III. http://tinyurl.com/3tgk3c9

[63] Having taught in both the United States and China, I believe that this tendency for self-knowledge, self-criticism, and deferral to expertise still permeates society. My students in China were far more aware of their faults than my American students. Moreover, my Chinese teachers were far more comfortable making comparisons between myself and my classmates in front of class, however painful it was for us.

ability? Indeed, how can we even classify it according to our traditional notions of the Separations of Power? A second difficulty for traditional Western notions of jurisprudence is the power of Dworkin's argument that we *need* a society of integrity and that the political virtue of integrity necessitates a *community*. He points to the fraternity of the French Revolution. I hope it is not too irreverent to point out that many countries in Europe, facing a crisis of community, are currently looking to the United States as a model of pluralistic harmony.

The moderate goal of this paper was simply this: the acknowledgment that we can look to China for help with these concerns. An analysis of the Chinese system of government leads to a number of surprising conclusions about why their bureaucracy was successful in harnessing the power of the elites: it was not just that they had a meritocracy, but they had a populace metaphysically prepared (via theological means) to accept the legitimacy of its rulers without democratic election. This system was based on a fundamentally un-American concept : that people are not at all equal, that they were indeed different in ability and virtue, and should be awarded political power accordingly.

This concept of empowering the intellectual elite through mericratic, objective, non-partisan means to handle the complex affairs of state should not surprise us; indeed, one might wonder why it took an Industrial Revolution for its necessity to be realized. As much as we would expect that a country implementing a democracy would look to the West, we might want to appeal to China for aid in constructing an effective bureaucracy and in analyzing its ramifications for issues like discretion and rule of law. Mencius is as important as Plato for any discussion of the Rule of Law, democracy, or idealism.

In this regard, I am personally astounded that the literati of the West have been so far behind the capitalists in seeking the treasures of China. The Confucian system that successfully blended a pragmatism rooted in the (astoundingly intuitive even for a postmodernist relativist) concept of family love, combined with Mencius's rigorous metaphysics, and then universalized and transmitted to the entire population with rites every bit as fluid and practicable as a religious rite must be recognized as the genius political work that it is. Moreover, anyone who is alarmed by the recent success of the "China Model" of government need not just look at the CCP, but also to Mencius, and to the Chinese people— a people, who, on further review, intangibly hold their leaders to a standard that exists despite the lack of democratic checks.

I believe that this phenomenon offers insight to some of the fundamental political and legal problems we face today (particularly when we are asking questions about institutions the Chinese have had for over 2,000 years), and should be pursued with the same rigor that jurists trace over the worn texts of the *Leviathan* and *Republic,* seeking to squeeze more inspiration out of them. It is my contention that Plato, at least, would have recognized this, but then again, he might have wanted to claim it as his own.

NIETZSCHE, NATURAL LAW, AND THE RESHAPING OF *PHYSIS*
Yunus Tuncel

The theory of natural law has shaped the Occidental legal and ethical discourse in many different ways. Although Thomas Aquinas is considered to be its best representative, many of its presuppositions precede his writings and exist in Greek and Roman thought, especially in Aristotle and Stoicism. In the modern age, on the other hand, the theory has taken a new shape, a "secular" form, so to speak, and is expressed by political thinkers such as Hobbes and Locke, who reflect on new forms of cohesion under the rubric of social contract theory. The purpose of this essay is not to study all these ideas on natural law, but rather to explore how Nietzsche would approach the theory of natural law and critique some of its presuppositions and building blocks. Although the natural law takes up an important space in the history of Western philosophy[1] and although Nietzsche engages in a polemical discussion with many ideas in this history, the natural law theory is not one of them. Or, better said, Nietzsche does not engage in an extensive polemic directly on natural law. However, many of the presuppositions of natural law in any of its formulations are undermined by Nietzsche's critique, especially in his late writings, as in *Beyond Good and Evil* and elsewhere. What follows is first an examination and a reconstruction of his critique and then a presentation of Nietzsche's conception of nature, which can be read as an alternative idea to natural law.[2]

---

[1] For a brief survey of the natural law theory in the history of philosophy, see Plouffe's essay in *Vera Lex* 9. 1 & 2 (2008): 77-121.

[2] While doing this examination of Nietzsche on natural law, we must place epochal issues between brackets. To put it simply, the death of God signifies a turning point in Nietzsche's world-view and opens up new horizons in the formation of a new epoch. While natural law and its underlying premises belong to the old, Godly epoch, which Nietzsche often refers to as the "morality of good and evil," a confrontation with them is necessary especially because they still play some role in different aspects of contemporary society. The bell started ringing in 1882, but there are still many who have yet to hear it.

I. NIETZSCHE ON NATURAL LAW

According to Nietzsche, natural law is a superstition:

> *Law of nature's a superstition.*— When you speak so rapturously of a conformity to law in nature you must either assume that all natural things freely obey laws they themselves have imposed upon themselves — in which case you are admiring the morality of nature — or you are entranced by the idea of a creative mechanic who has made the most ingenious clock, with living creatures upon it as decorations. — Necessity in nature becomes more human and a last refuge of mythological dreaming through the expression 'conformity to law.'[3]

We do not know yet the full scope of Nietzsche's problematization of natural law, but what this early passage indicates is that it is a fantastic projection of human dreaming: we either like to see morality in nature or we are impressed by the creator of nature. In either case, a certain conception of nature is assumed within the scheme of such a metaphysics.[4] According to Aristotle, who gives us a coherent conception of nature, nature is that which is self-created as opposed to those things that are produced by humans; in the former the principle of production is in the things themselves whereas in the latter that principle comes from outside. "A nature, then, is what we have said; and the things that have a nature are those that have this sort of principle. All these things are substances; for <a substance> is a sort of subject, and a nature is invariably in a subject. The things that are

---

[3] *Assorted Opinions and Maxims*, tr. R. J. Hollingdale, (Cambridge: Cambridge University Press, 1986), Aphorism 9, 216.

[4] Nietzsche's critique of Western metaphysics, which starts with *Human, All Too Human*, is too broad a subject to bring up here. Many of his points, however, are applicable to Aristotle's metaphysics. A succinct critique is presented in "The Four Great Errors" of the *Twilight of the Idols*: first, the confusion of cause and effect, which Nietzsche calls "the real corruption of reason." Second, the error of false causality, which applies to causation in human action, as Nietzsche puts it: "… a doer (a "subject") was slipped under all that happened." Third, the error of imaginary causes in which a cause is placed after the fact; this is because of the causal instinct that always wants an explanation. Nietzsche then goes on to explain the psychology of this imaginary causality in which he claims that a particular cause that is comforting dominates the scene of causality.

in accordance with nature include both these and whatever belongs to them in their own right…" (*Physics*, Book II, sec.1, 192b 30-35) No doubt, in Aristotle nature is said in many different ways, not to mention the complication that ensues from the specific and the generic use of the word. Nature is connected to substance, but they are not the same; substance is what remains continuously. Moreover, nature has within itself a principle of motion and change. Finally, nature is the shape and form of things and the form is the nature more than the matter is.[5] In Aristotle, nature is intricately connected to his conception of causality. And this conception of nature is also transplanted onto Aristotle's ethics and politics in which there is a natural justice[6] and a natural law (a "common" law according to nature[7]), which stands above particular laws of city-states. Although Aristotle may be the first known metaphysician of nature, he does not develop a comprehensive natural law theory.

In a similar vein, the Stoics use a certain conception of nature, as intricately linked to their understanding of creation ordained by a supernatural rational being, consequently with more emphasis than Aristotle on its transcendental affixture. Living according to nature becomes their dictum, which presupposes a pre-determined place for all beings that exist in accordance with this divine plan and a blind acceptance of one's fate, one's god-given place on earth. "Be content with what is given and pray to the gods;" that is what the Stoics upheld. In the dictum "live according to nature" Nietzsche saw a projection, an idealization. "'According to nature' you want to *live*? O you noble Stoics, what deceptive words these are! Imagine being like nature, wasteful beyond measure, indifferent beyond measure, without purposes and consideration, without mercy and justice, fertile and desolate…how *could* you live according to this indifference?"[8] There is no nature as such for Nietzsche; the Stoic

---

[5] Aristotle, *Physics* Book II.
[6] Aristotle, *Nicomachean Ethics*, Book V.
[7] Aristotle, *Rhetoric*
[8] *Beyond Good and Evil* in *Basic Writings of Nietzsche*, tr. W. Kaufmann (New York: The

reads into nature what he idealizes, how he would like to see the order of things to be. "Your pride wants to impose your morality, your ideal, on nature …"[9] While exposing how partial philosophers are—they are also all too human—when they regard existence, Nietzsche also reveals power structures that are hidden in such schemes of interpretation: "Philosophy is this tyrannical drive itself, the most spiritual will to power."[10] More will be said on the question of power later.

One sees the culmination of Stoic teachings on natural law in Cicero's works. In *De Legibus*, Cicero argues that law cannot begin with human beings but rather with a higher power that dictates over them. This is why he starts, via Marcus in the dialogue, by defining law as "a certain eternal principle, which governs the entire universe; wisely commanding what is right, and prohibiting what is wrong. Therefore, that aboriginal and supreme law is the Spirit of God himself; enjoining virtue, and restraining vice. It is for this reason that this law, which the gods have bestowed on the human race, is so justly applauded. For it is the reason and mind of Wisdom, urging us to good, and deterring us from evil."[11] According to this Stoic conception of law, not only reason is projected back into the universe and its creator, but also law (which originally could have meant custom, rule, or tradition, as in Greek *nomos*), has now collapsed into a limited reading of political and moral law that is supposed to maintain and ascertain social order. What ensues in this dialogue is a clear demarcation between eternal law/natural law and human law. Human commandments and prohibitions do not have sufficient moral power, but should receive their guidance from higher, divine power. "The moral power of law, is not only far more ancient than these legal institutions of states and peoples, but it is coeval with God himself, who beholds and governs both heaven and

---

Modern Library, 1992), Aphorism 9, 205-6.
[9] *Ibid.*
[10] *Ibid.*
[11] *De Legibus*, Book II.

earth. For it is impossible that the divine mind should exist without reason; and divine reason must necessarily be possessed of a power to determine what is virtuous and what is vicious."[12] In order to be true or to approximate true laws, human laws must be attuned to Divine Reason, *ratio divina*, and be in conformity with nature: "For law is the just distinction between right and wrong, conformable to nature, the original and principal regulator of all things, by which the laws of men should be measured, whether they punish the guilty or protect the innocent."[13]

More than a millennium after Cicero, Aquinas appropriates Greek and Roman ideas within the context of Christian theology and Aristotelian revivalism. Before his well-known treatise on law, Aquinas reflects on natural justice by way of Aristotle's *Nicomachean Ethics*: According to its effect and power, "it [justice] is natural, has the same force and power everywhere." This is based on the presupposition that "nature is the same everywhere among all men." According to its cause, on the other hand, "legal or positive justice always has its origin in natural justice."[14] For Nietzsche, nature is not and cannot be the same everywhere—because this would mean that nature is static, unchanging (an idea that is also contra early Greek thought); in addition, this presupposition relies on a chain of false causality.[15] On the contrary, "all laws of nature are relations."[16] Even in early Nietzsche, we see an attempt to overturn the metaphysics of natural law.[17] Instead of a causality that posits a cause behind every

[12] *Ibid.*
[13] *Ibid.*
[14] *Commentary on Aristotle's Nicomachean Ethics*, 440-441.
[15] For Nietzsche on false causality, see "The Four Great Errors" in *Twilight of the Idols* in *Portable Nietzsche*, tr. W. Kaufmann (New York: Penguin Books, 1954), 492-501.
[16] *Kritische Studienausgabe*, KS from hereafter (Berlin: De Guyter, 1999), 493 (translation is mine).
[17] Roughly in the same period, Nietzsche exposes the archaic religious layers in the genealogy of natural law. Initially there is no uniformity or regularity in nature; this is the case in human prehistory, but then at some stage of human development nature becomes uniform: "In those ages one as yet knows nothing of natural laws … Any conception of *natural* causality is altogether lacking … The whole of nature is in the conception of religious men a sum of actions by conscious and volitional beings, a tremendous complex

effect, Nietzsche sees a relationality among beings, which does not isolate the interpreter from the *interpretans*. "Every law of nature is, first and foremost, a sum of anthropological relations."[18] This metaphysical isolation lies at the root of positing the interpreter, the rational agent, as the hegemonic ruler over "nature," as the *interpretans*. Now let us see the role of rationality in natural law.

In his well-known "Treatise on Law," this is how Aquinas defines natural law: "They [rational creatures] participate in eternal reason in that they have a natural inclination to their proper actions and ends. Such participation in the eternal law by rational creatures is called the natural law."[19] As he presents his four-part conception of law, Aquinas not only emphasizes the rational aspect of being human, but also prioritizes rational creatures over other types of creatures. This emphasis and prioritization is based on Aquinas' conception of human that is borrowed from Greek metaphysics: a

---

of *arbitrariness*. In regard to everything external to us no conclusion can be drawn that something *will* be thus or thus, *must* happen thus or thus; it is *we* who are the more or less secure and calculable; man is the *rule*, nature is *irregularity*—this proposition contains the fundamental conviction which dominates rude, religiously productive primitive cultures. We men of today feel precisely the opposite: the richer a man feels within himself, the more polyphonic his subjectivity is, the more powerfully is he impressed by the uniformity of nature ..." There arises the need, in the archaic human, to impose regularity and uniformity on nature, which, among others, is a problem of power: "How can one exercise an influence over these terrible unknown powers, how can one fetter the domain of freedom? thus he asked himself, thus he anxiously seeks: are there then no means of regulating these powers through a tradition and law in just the way you are regulated by them? — The believer in magic and miracles reflects on how to *impose a law on nature* — : and, in brief, the religious cult is the outcome of this reflection." *Human, All Too Human*, tr. R. J. Hollingdale, (Cambridge: Cambridge University Press, 1986), Aphorism 111, 63-65. Based on this and other reflections by Nietzsche on natural law, we can conclude that there are major layers that lie in the genealogy of natural law: archaic irregular (lawless) nature; religious cults and the desire to bring regularity to nature; the first conceptualization of nature as in early Greek thought (the turning point in philosophical terms); metaphysics of nature in later Greek thought (the first formulations of natural law); Roman adaptation for practical purposes of ruling; medieval version as integrated into Christian theology; and finally modern secular version (which will be discussed below).

[18] *Ibid.*, 494 (translation is mine).

[19] *St. Thomas Aquinas on Politics and Ethics*, tr. P. E. Sigmund (New York: W. W. Norton, 1988), 46.

human being is essentially a rational being. "Thus the proposition, "Man is a rational being" is by its nature self-evident since when we say "man" we are also saying "rational,"[20] This reduction, or essentialization, of a human being to its capacity to think—to turn a part into a whole, to speak the metaphysician's language—has come under close scrutiny in Nietzsche's works from the beginning to the end. Although Nietzsche's criticism of Occidental logocentricity is general, as it targets a tradition that spans from Socrates to Kant and Hegel, and does not mention Aquinas anywhere in this regard, it can be applied to the Thomistic conception of natural law. For Nietzsche the excessive reliance on and use of reason, which he calls "the *hypertrophy*"[21] of the logical instinct as he sees in the type of theoretical man that Socrates represents, leads to the decline of culture, the demise of the Dionysian along with mythic, poetic, and artistic forces, the emaciation of the body and all bodily regimes, all of which are symptomatic of Aquinas' Christian world-view. In short, natural law, for Nietzsche, would be a symptom of the decline of life forces.

Furthermore, this theory of natural law is reinforced by two more points in Aquinas. First, natural inclinations; all human beings have natural inclination towards the good. Aquinas expands this point by connecting the natural law to such things as self-preservation, procreation, education, and knowledge of God, all of which are based on the idea of the good.[22] Second, the natural law is the same for all humans as far as its general first principles are concerned.[23] Both of these points fall within the framework of what Nietzsche calls "mo-

---

[20] *Ibid.*, 49.

[21] "Specifically, we observe here a monstrous *defectus* of any mystical disposition, so Socrates might be called the typical *non-mystic*, in whom, through a hypertrophy, the logical nature is developed as excessively as instinctive wisdom is in the mystic." *The Birth of Tragedy* in the *Basic Writings of Nietzsche*, 88.

[22] *St. Thomas Aquinas on Politics and Ethics*, 49-50.

[23] *Ibid.*, p.51. Here Aquinas states that "the natural law is the same for all, both as a standard of right action and as to the possibility that it can be known." He then adds that there are exceptions when one's reason is corrupted by passion, bad habit, or an evil disposition of nature, all of which are contrary to the law of nature.

rality of good and evil," sometimes simply "morality," with which he refers to the highest values that have shaped the Occidental civilization since the Socratic Greeks. Nietzsche takes philosophers to task for having dogmatically established or attempted to establish such a foundation, a foundation of first principles, and for having baptized it as Truth. Some of the problems Nietzsche exposes in the philosophical tradition are: first, philosophers, in their zeal for truth, have been blinded to the problem of untruth (error, illusion, deception, falsity, fantasy, etc.).[24] Second, philosophers are not honest enough in their work; they confuse truth with truthfulness (i.e. the search for truth),[25] which is analogous to calling a journey the last stop. Third, they project their own ideals onto nature and define nature as such,[26] a problem that was presented above by way of Stoicism. Fourth, such projections are expressions of their will to power,[27] their desire to be the masters of the world, but they hide such desire, this will to power. Fifth, philosophers are blinded to what language, their basic medium, is and how it functions.[28] Sixth, philosophers have emphasized conscious and abstract forms[29] of thinking to the neglect of unconscious and intuitive forms. The problems of philosophers are endless,[30] but we must end the list with one more point: philosophers despise the body and the senses[31] and have understood them only poorly.

The errors of philosophers, specifically in the conceptions of nature and natural law, continue in the modern age despite the many discontinuities that lie in the shift from the Medieval epoch to moder-

---

[24] *Beyond Good and Evil*, sections 1-4, in *Basic Writings of Nietzsche*, 199-202.
[25] *Ibid.*, section 5, 202.
[26] *Ibid.*, section 9.
[27] *Ibid.*, sections 13 and 23.
[28] *Ibid.*, sections 16-21.
[29] *Ibid.*, section 16.
[30] I have focused on the problems of philosophers as Nietzsche discusses them in *Beyond Good and Evil*; another good source to add to the list is *Twilight of the Idols*.
[31] *Ibid.*, sec.15. For a lengthy discussion of this topic in Nietzsche, see his *On the Genealogy of Morals*, especially the Third Essay, and "Anti-Nature Morality" in the *Twilight of the Idols*.

nity. Early modern philosophers grapple with the task of establishing new binding principles. For instance, Hobbes, in his formulation of a social contract theory, takes the law of nature as the foundation of a viable, peaceful society that is diametrically opposed to the state of nature. Law of nature, or natural law, for Hobbes is: "a precept, or general rule, found out by reason, by which a man is forbidden to do that which is destructive of his life, or takes away the means of preserving the same; and to omit that by which he thinks it may best be preserved."[32] All specific laws of nature, nineteen in total, are derived from this first rational principle. Again a rational foundation is established by Hobbes for the new binding principles, although it is removed from the ideals of perfection, happiness, and after-life. According to Nietzsche, Hobbes too succumbs to the 'problem of morality itself; what was lacking was any suspicion that there was something problematic here. What the philosophers called "a rational foundation of morality" and tried to supply was, seen in the right light, merely a scholarly variation of the common *faith* in the prevalent morality…'[33] Hobbes, too, is a variation on the main melody and is not a radical departure from the metaphysics of natural law.

In conclusion, for Nietzsche the different theories of natural law, which may constitute one tradition despite its theistic/atheistic and medieval/secular variations, are expressions of the will to power of their authors and interpretations. It is not a matter of "fact" or "text"; rather, an "emendation and perversion of meaning." Some others may come along and interpret something else, some opposing principles, out of "nature": "But as said above, that is interpretation, not text; and somebody might come along who, with opposite intentions and modes of interpretation, could read out of the same "nature," and with regard to the same phenomena, rather the tyrannically inconsiderate and relentless enforcement of claims of power…"[34] If it is all interpretation—and not all interpretations are equal in Ni-

---

[32] Hobbes, *Leviathan*, pt. 1, ch. 14, 64.
[33] *Beyond Good and Evil* in *Basic Writings*, 287-289.
[34] *Ibid.*, 220-1.

etzsche—what then becomes for him the criteria for that which is binding? Nietzsche's conception of dynamic nature may shed light on this question.

II. NATURE IN NIETZSCHE: *PHYSIS* AS SELF-TRANSFORMATION

In contrast to the metaphysics of nature as briefly outlined above along with its problems, Nietzsche does not have a static or a causal understanding of nature or an understanding of law, in the broad sense, based on such a conception. Since for Nietzsche the emphasis has shifted to the individual, nature is understood within the context of one's growth, as in *physis*, and one's self-overcoming as one is embedded in one's history and environment. Nietzsche's paradigm for participation or becoming a member of a community (or creating any collectivities) is based on this idea of self-overcoming; what one may call a "Dionysian individualism." In what follows I will discuss four related topics in Nietzsche's conception of nature: physiological aspect of nature; transformation of one's nature; mastery of drives and character; and nature as being sovereign.

Physiology. From the beginning to the end of his philosophical life Nietzsche persistently questions how the body, our inheritance from the living world, plays a crucial role in our entire being, including the way we speak and think. A note from his early period testifies to this: "All inclination, friendship, love, at the same time, something physiological. We do not know all, how deep and high *physis* reaches."[35] Through our body, the body that grows and is ever-changing, we are connected to all the living beings and all existence in general; for example, the satyr, an emphatic human/animal body, plays the role of a bridge between the human world and all existence in Greek tragedy. While bringing to light the problems of despising the body,[36] Nietzsche at the same time shows

[35] KS 7, 407 (translation is mine).
[36] See the section "On the Despisers of the Body" in *Thus Spoke Zarathustra* in *Portable Nietzsche*, pp.146-7.

how the body lies, often unconsciously, at the root of our being and acting. The body is a multiplicity, a battle-ground for drives and instincts; to know one's self, one must *know* one's body in its multiplicity. Moreover, Nietzsche brings to the foreground the question of the senses; there may be an agreement here with the empiricists on their emphasis on the senses, although Nietzsche goes beyond the epistemological domain and promotes an understanding of each sense—how poorly we *understand* the sense of smelling, for instance—and of all the senses working together synaesthetically. Finally, Nietzsche, in his critical evaluation of chastity[37] and the ascetic ideal and in anticipation of Freudian psychoanalysis, stresses the importance of sexuality. In "Morality as Anti-nature"[38] Nietzsche critiques Christian morality for having fought passion with excision and for having condemned the instincts, while praising, in "What I Owe to the Ancients," the ancients for having embraced the Dionysian:

> For it is only in the Dionysian mysteries, in the psychology of the Dionysian state, that the basic fact of the Hellenic instinct finds expression—its "will to live." What was it that the Hellene guaranteed himself by means of these mysteries? Eternal life, the eternal return of life; the future promised and hallowed in the past; the triumphant Yes to life beyond all death and change; true life as the overall continuation of life through procreation, through the mysteries of sexuality. For the Greeks the sexual symbol was therefore the venerable symbol par excellence, the real profundity in the whole of ancient piety.[39]

Transformation of one's nature. Despite his rejection of otherworldly principles, Nietzsche does not dismiss the fact that human beings lie on the chain of what is given to them in history: "For

---

[37] *Ibid.*, pp. 166-7: "Those for whom chastity is difficult should be counseled against it, lest it become their road to hell…" This may be a warning sign to those who still cling to the ideal of chastity.

[38] *Twilight of the Idols* in *Portable Nietzsche*, pp.486-492.

[39] *Ibid.*, 560-563.

since we are the outcome of earlier generations, we are also the outcome of their aberrations, passions and errors, and indeed of their crimes; it is not possible wholly to free oneself from this chain."[40] This chain, however, is not an unbroken or an unbreakable hegemony. One can, to the extent that one knows one's history, break out of this hegemony and recreate oneself, both in the individual and the collective sense. For this one needs to develop a second *physis* that will allow the first *physis* to die; a new tradition replacing the old one, so to speak. "The best we can do is to confront our inherited and hereditary nature with our knowledge of it, and through a new, stern discipline combat our inborn heritage and implant in ourselves a new habit, a new instinct, a second nature, so that our first nature withers away."[41] A model of transformation that operates with the model of *historical unconsciousness* is presented here based on a conception of ever-changing nature. But we must not forget the emphasis on "stern discipline" which takes us to the next issue.

Mastery. Having mastery over one's self is a theme that appears frequently in Nietzsche. In his early works it appears as an Apollonian function, *Bändigung*, setting limits, drawing the boundaries for oneself, a crucial function that is operative in cult practices and *freedoms*. In this sense, it also means knowing oneself, one's weaknesses and strengths, one's own archetype and type, and one's capacity to suffer. Nietzsche shows not only why mastery is needed for character development and greatness but also how mastery works in the creation of morality. "Every morality is, as opposed to *laisser aller* [letting go], a bit of tyranny against 'nature'; also against 'reason'; but this in itself is no objection..."[42] While showing how mastery works over "nature" in general, Nietzsche is careful in making a distinction between the type of mastery that artists use in their creative acts and the type of mastery that limits horizons and

---

[40] *Untimely Meditation*, tr. R. J. Hollingdale (Cambridge: Cambridge University Press, 1983), 76.
[41] *Ibid.*
[42] *Beyond Good and Evil* in *Basic Writings*, p.290.

perspectives and is used for taming and disciplining. "Every artist knows how far from any feeling of letting himself go his 'most natural' state is … and how strictly and subtly he obeys thousand-fold laws precisely then…" On the other hand, "consider any morality with this in mind: what there is in it of 'nature' teaches hatred of the *laisser aller*, of any all-too-great freedom, and implants the need for limited horizons and the nearest tasks—teaching the *narrowing of our perspective*, and thus in a certain sense stupidity, as a condition of life and growth."[43] In this way, such moralities go against *physis* or growing and life forces, because they narrow perspectives, they deny the validity of other truths and other ways of being. In short, they are reactive and life-negating and deny "all-too-great freedom." This idea of freedom connects us to the spirit of Nietzsche's sovereign individual.

Sovereignty. In his critique of the process of civilization, Nietzsche traces the origin of conscience to the dominant instinct of the sovereign individual.[44] But who is Nietzsche's sovereign individual? He appears at the end of the civilized process and is liberated from the morality of custom: "in short, the man who has his own independent, protracted will and the *right to make promises*—and in him a proud consciousness … of *what* has at length been achieved and become flesh in him, a consciousness of his own power and freedom, a sensation of mankind come to completion."[45] This is not the Kantian autonomous individual who acts under the principle of equality and reciprocity, but rather an autonomous type that masters over himself and over others: "how should he not be aware of his superiority over all those who lack the right to make promises and stand as their own guarantors…"[46] This *inequality* under the *law*, law as highest value, marks a clear separation between Nietzsche and those theorists of natural law for whom all souls or citizens are

---

[43] *Ibid.*, pp.291-2.
[44] *On the Genealogy of Morals*, Second Essay, Sec.2 in *Basic Writings*, 494-6.
[45] *Ibid.*
[46] *Ibid.*

equal. "...how this mastery over himself also necessarily gives him mastery over circumstances, over nature, and over all more short-willed and unreliable creatures? The "free" man ... also possesses his *measure of value* ..."[47] By way of a specific type of *naturalism*, Nietzsche is expounding his ideas on value and value-creation, more specifically *who* these value-creators are. It is "the consciousness of this rare freedom, this power over oneself and over fate" that makes the value-creator. And he stamps his civilization with "conscience," as the mark of his own *physis*-governed values.

In conclusion of this part, physiological states, self-transformation, mastery over oneself and sovereignty form the four corner stones from which we can interrogate Nietzsche on his conception of *physis* which, in many ways, offers an alternative, an *an-archic* model to the theory of natural law.

EPILOGUE

For Nietzsche the discussion on law, *lex* as the substantive of *ligare,* turns into a discussion on value. He could have used the term 'law' (*Gesetz*) in the sense of *nomos*, but more often than not, he uses the term 'value' (*Werte*), sometimes 'highest value,' in order to move the discussion onto a broader and deeper plain. We are not shaped, bound, and governed only by laws that appear to be laws, but rather, and more importantly, by highest values that are often invisible and that lie behind, at the root of what are considered to be laws. Nietzsche's task was to expose these highest values and to show how and why they fail to be *binding* values. Some of these problematic values in Occidental history are overestimation of reason, devaluation of the body and the senses, foundationalism or belief in Truth (what he calls "will to truth), and false causality; these are also the building blocks of the theory of natural law. I do not think Nietzsche calls for an end of discussion on issues concerning moral, legal and political theory, but rather for a change in the

[47] *Ibid.*

rules of the game so that such debates take place within the context of invisible and deeper highest values that have remained beyond the gaze of previous philosophers. Since Nietzsche many thinkers have embarked on different journeys to explore different aspects of "binding under the law," not law as Truth, but rather as *truthful*, while they have given much thought, directly or indirectly, to the question of nature, nature as "transformed and transforming *physis*," and how human beings may remain truthful to their singular natures and yet form meaningful bonds that sustain them together.

BOOK REVIEWS

FUNDAMENTALISM: THE SEARCH FOR MEANING
By Malise Ruthven, Oxford University Press, 2004
Reviewed by Peter P. Cvek
Department of Philosophy
Saint Peter's College

The term "fundamentalism" came into common use in the early part of the twentieth century, having been adopted by some evangelical Protestants in the United States, who sought to defend what they took to be the "fundamentals" of their Christian beliefs and way of life against the rise of modernism and the increased secularization of American culture. Since that time, the term has been applied to movements within almost every major religious tradition, from Christian, Islamic and Jewish fundamentalism to Hindu, Sikh, and Buddhist variants, making fundamentalism a world-wide phenomenon. In this rather condensed study, Malise Ruthven, a scholar of Islamic studies and a former script writer for the BBC, aims at uncovering the core meaning of contemporary religious fundamentalism. Adopting Wittgenstein's concept of "family resemblances," Ruthven seeks to identify a network of overlapping similarities and parallels between the so-called fundamentalisms of different religious traditions. In attempting to unpack the meaning of what he likes to call "the F-word," Ruthven explores a number of family resemblances, including the scandal of differences, the snares of literalism, the treatment of women, and the potent connection between fundamentalism and nationalism.

Broadly construed, fundamentalism may be described as "a religious way of being that manifests itself in a strategy by which beleaguered believers attempt to preserve their distinctive identity as a people or group in the face of modernity and secularization" (8).

In contrast with traditionalism, fundamentalism may be described as "tradition made self-aware and consequently defensive" (17). Ruthven deftly develops this theme under the heading of the scandal of difference. In so far as pluralism is an integral feature of modernity, fundamentalism is "one response to the crisis of faith brought about by the awareness of differences" (47). The fundamentalist is scandalized by these differences, which are experienced as shocking and offensive. At this level, the logic of fundamentalism is simple enough. Commitment to the truth of one's own tradition necessarily excludes the alleged truths of any other tradition. This is said to be especially true of the western monotheistic traditions, where doctrinal confessions appear to be mutually exclusive. Such exclusivity rubs against the grain of increasing globalization and pluralism. For the fundamentalist, however, pluralism leads to relativism, the enemy of absolutism and truth (47). Moreover, "the encroachments of modernity through state power and state bureaucracies are pervasive and continuous and a constant challenge to all religious traditions" (57). But while traditionalists, like the Amish, remain passive, the fundamentalist is an activist who refuses to retreat into isolation. Fundamentalism is "seldom content with defending its minority status against the onslaught of a pluralistic, secular world, it strives to 'fight back' by exercising power, directly or indirectly" (57).

Fundamentalism is often associated with a literal interpretation of religious texts. But, as Ruthven points out, since these texts seldom lend themselves to mechanical literalism, the real issue is inerrancy. Sacred texts provide the authoritative raft of dogmatic truth and certainty in a sea of conflicting opinions and ideologies, while the assumption of inerrancy allows for a more selective and flexible interpretation of these texts. In an effort to extend the fundamentalist label beyond evangelical Christians and Islamic conservatives to traditional minded Roman Catholics, Ruthven substitutes the doctrine of papal infallibility for that of biblical inerrancy (61).

Despite the problematic extension of the fundamentalist label beyond the textually based Abrahamic religious tradition, at least two "family resemblances" provide the basis for including Hindu fundamentalism among contemporary religious fundamentalists: the treatment of women and the melding of religion with nationalism. Ruthven begins his discussion of the former with the revival of the ritual of sati: the ceremonial act by which a widow is burned on her husband's funeral pyre. He observes that "the pro-sati agitation can be seen as part of a counter-feminist or patriarchal protest movement that is common among fundamentalists in all traditions" (102). As Ruthven sees it, Hindu fundamentalists, like all fundamentalists, are preoccupied not only with sexuality, but more particularly, with the expression of female sexuality. Of the more than 195 provisions introduced to codify Islamic law in the Islamic Republic of Iran, according to Ruthven, 107 articles were concerned with the regulation of sexual activities, ranging from the prosecution of adultery and homosexuality to prohibiting unrelated persons of the same sex from lying naked under the same blanket (103). Jewish and Christian fundamentalists are painted with the same brush. Generally speaking, fundamentalists reject the legal equality of men and women, exclude women from most leadership positions, express concern about the content of female sexuality, and strictly distinguish between male and female roles. All fundamentalists are opposed to homosexuality. Since they came into being in a time when human survival depended on the maintenance of a strict division between male and female roles, Ruthven suggests that all major religious traditions are fundamentally patriarchal (114).

It is certainly the case that fundamentalists oppose the sexual revolution and the full liberation of women. Whether patriarchy is an inherent part of most religious traditions is debatable. But Ruthven's foray into simplistic psychoanalytic interpretations of Catholicism and anti-homosexuality is even more suspect. According to Ruthven, this specific instance of homophobia is rooted in the efforts to avoid the contradiction between the ideal of heterosexuality and the expectation "to love a solitary deity imagined in terms both of father imagery, and perhaps more potently, through the erotically charged figure of a young, almost naked male impaled on an instrument of torment" (122). Homophobia, according to Ruthven, resolves the contradiction between homoerotic religious feelings and heterosexual social values. Even if this had explanatory value in the case of Catholicism, which is doubtful, it would not seem to apply to many other religious traditions.

Finally and most importantly is the connection that has been forged between fundamentalism and nationalism. In so far as nationalism is typically construed as a function of progressive modern ideologies, it would appear that nationalism would be at odds with fundamentalism. But, following the work of Juergensmeyer and Mircea Eliade, Ruthven views secular nationalism as having many of the characteristics of a religion, including doctrine, myths, ethics, ritual experiences, and social organization (143). Both nationalism and religion provide a framework of moral order and a guide for action, and most significantly, both can provide a sanction for violence and martyrdom (143). This is especially true where religious identity is already associated with national identity, an association which has often had disastrous consequences around the world.

Christian fundamentalists in America, for example, see no conflict between religion and patriotism; identifying America with biblical Israel, they understand the nation's history and greatness in terms of a special covenant with God, which is conditional on obedience to a divinely ordained moral order (129). They view the perceived decline in American stature and prosperity as the just consequences of secular America's failure to live up to that covenant, and call for a return to God and to an idolized past (the 1950s or even the period of the founding fathers) when traditional values ruled the day. This "myth of a golden age," when the religious and moral norms of the tradition prevailed, is another common feature of fundamentalist ideology (41). In contrast with more spiritual interpretations of a return to origins, fundamentalists actively seek to bring about this restoration. Unfortunately, this goal often brings them into conflict with those who do not share their ideals.

The parallels with other fundamentalist movements are intriguing. Islamic fundamentalists, reacting to the humiliations of colonialism and the corruption of the postcolonial era, seek a return to the glory days of triumphal Islam and the period of Rightly Guided Caliphs (131). In so far as this decline in fortune is attributed to a loss of faith among Muslims, especially Muslim rulers who do not rule in accordance with the Koran, only a return to the strict adherents to Islamic law will turn the tide. Of course, efforts to achieve this end often clash with the more secular character of post-colonial governments. In contrast with secular Zionists and even some orthodox Jewish groups, religious Zionists understand the return to Israel as the redemption of the Jewish people and a re-appropriation of the land bequeathed to them by God. This process is often envisioned as a return to the era of David and Solomon and the restoration of the First Temple in Jerusalem, a restoration that would require the destruction of the Dome of the Rock and the al-Aqsa mosque. (42). Despite the apparent lack of canonical scriptures and the pluralistic character of Indian religious life, the emergence of Hindu fundamentalism is a function of its efforts to unite Indian and Hindu identities. The Hindu nationalist movement in India similarly treats the ancient Vedic texts as authoritative and promotes a return to the values of the Vedic age. This sense of return was poignantly illustrated by the attempt to rebuild Ram's temple at Ayodhya after the demolition of the mosque on the same site (42).

This well regarded book is an invaluable introduction to the rise and development of fundamentalism among some of the major religions of the world. First published in 2004, this text has appropriately been re-issued by Oxford as part of its "very short introduction" series. Ruthven's identification of the overlapping ideas and themes inherent in contemporary fundamentalism is illuminating and often provocative. Nevertheless, one still finds that something is missing from this account. Ruthven's search for the meaning of fundamentalism belies the fact that fundamentalism itself is a search for meaning, a search which takes place in a modern world that offers very little to satisfy the soul beyond consumerism and the superficial pursuit of hedonistic satisfaction. This deeper search for meaning is not part of Ruthven's analysis. For those like Ruthven, who assumed that "modernization and secularization were inexorably connected," the very existence of fundamentalism is both baffling and disappointing (196). Warnings about the dangers of fundamentalist ideologies, especially when they serve as the basis for violence and inhumanity, cannot be underestimated. Yet, Ruthven tends to treat all but the most tamed and docile expressions of religious belief as obstacles to the eventual triumph of liberal secularism. Whatever else can be said about this clash of cultures, Ruthven would have to concede that the reports about the death of God have been greatly exaggerated.

THE BOURGEOIS VIRTUES
By Deirdre McCloskey, University of Chicago Press, 2006
Reviewed by Richard Connerney
Department of Philosophy & Religious Studies
Pace University, New York

I turned to Deirdre McCloskey's *The Bourgeois Virtues* for some good news about capitalism; something many people would like to hear these days. Dishonest corporate executives, deceptive advertisements, faulty products and predatory lending are some of the usual complaints about our financial system. On a deeper level, questions loom about the moral ecology our economic life engenders. Has capitalism and the technology it spawns, with its endless stream of pornographic images and Internet gambling sites available at the click of a mouse around the clock, its horrific economic crimes committed anonymously by remote, faceless con men, and its deliberate cultivation of covetousness, created an environment in which morality is a near impossibility?

McCloskey answers with an emphatic "No." Capitalism, in her view, has provided the human race with a rise in population, health, wealth and yes, virtue. Not only are we getting richer and more numerous, argues McCloskey, but we are improving ethically; capitalism is making us good-er. In her view the camel should, with a little lubricant and a running start, squeeze through the eye of the proverbial needle, as should the bourgeois society riding upon its back.

Those who would disagree with her find themselves on the wrong end of McCloskey's poison pen. To those who claim capitalism fractures human communities and creates isolation, McCloskey offers evidence to the contrary by deftly deconstructing the idea of ancient and pre-capitalist Edens of frictionless harmony. To ingrates who, since 1848, have questioned the ultimate value of capitalism, she offers a defense of the American bourgeoisie as better educated, better off and more social than his pre-capitalist predecessor.

Recent fiscal misbehavior is, in her view, not the result of capitalism per se, but an unbalanced variant of capitalism inspired by a tribe of acquisitive eggheads who promote bull-headed avarice as the dominant ethos. McCloskey terms this sub-species of capitalism as "Prudence-only" or simply "P" and she does an admirable job showing that such single-pointed reductionisms rarely describe commerce as it usually occurs. America is not and cannot be a nation motivated purely by money and even Wall Street at its worst reflects an aberrant mutation of our traditionally virtuous commercial habits.

P (prudence only) has always vied for preeminence with cultural, social and religious values (termed here S, or the sacred) as a motivation for our economic activity. S is both a cause and a consequence of capitalism's success. Honesty truly is the best policy for McCloskey; her ideal is a Jerry McGuire-like repudiation of unbridled greed for a capitalism that embraces love, hope and charity. This robust—or perhaps naive—optimism infuses *The Bourgeois Virtues*, which sometimes reads like a work of evangelism or an infomercial for an exercise machine: "By adopting the bourgeois virtues the Cubans, Haitians, North Koreans, Congolese, Sudanese, Myanmarians, and Zimbabweans can be enriched and liberated, as billions already have been." One wonders where to send your check for $29.95.

Clouds of doubt soon enter this sunny vision of capitalism, however. The reader wonders how McCloskey can claim that capitalism has enhanced the natural environment, "air quality has improved… in some respects in every rich city in the world," an incredible assertion for anyone who has spent an afternoon in Beijing. "Water service is better because half the world's population now has clean water piped into their homes," McCloskey continues undaunted. Mentions of looming water shortages, failing fish stocks, global warming and anxieties over the long-term viability of fossil fuels find no place in *The Bourgeois Virtues*.

In a work of such wide scope, the reader can forgive a few wild statements, but bizarre pronouncements occur on almost every page of *The Bourgeois Virtues*. To take but one example, McCloskey holds Calcutta up as an example of pre-capitalist desperation.

> I have emphasized that all our ancestors were poor, that everyone descends overwhelmingly from poor people, even slaves, since almost all societies before the eighteenth century...were by your standards and mine astoundingly poor. Try to imagine living on one dollar a day, with the prices of food and clothing and housing as they now are. Imagine, if you wish, an economy with very many such people, and so having commercial provision for mats to sleep hundreds abreast on the streets of Calcutta and for rice-by-the-bowl with pebbles and clay mixed in.

Never mind that before the arrival of the quintessentially capitalist British East India Company the city of Calcutta did not exist. Never mind that the teeming millions in contemporary India cannot possibly be our ancestors. Forget, if you can, that those huddled masses result from the massive growth in population that McCloskey, just a few pages earlier, holds up as proof of the triumph of capitalism. Just be happy you are not in Calcutta on a mat, and thank capitalism—however you may formulate it.

Punctuating these suspect statements is McCloskey's favorite refrain, "consider that you are mistaken." Weber, Marx, and Francis Fukuyama all receive the same perfunctory treatment as does natural law theory, which McCloskey dispatches with a sentence and a footnote, equating it with the phrase "homosexuality is bad." The frustrating part of all this is that McCloskey sometimes seems to be nearing a viable point and then sabotages herself with another bloviation. The combination of wild statements with summary dismissals of all who oppose her gives the reader the impression he has gone down the rabbit hole; the charges are nonsense but the Red Queen (or perhaps the Red Scare Queen) still calls for our heads.

The more serious problem with this book is its argumentation. McCloskey's central point—capitalism makes us more virtuous—suffers from two problems: the author does not clearly define capitalism and fails to define virtue. She admits to being "wishy-washy" and "loose and baggy" about her definitions, citing Kwame Anthony Appiah as a precedent. This allows for a pleasant flow in the language of the book, as McCloskey flits effortlessly between eras and economic philosophers. The end result of this approach, however, is that she has excused *The Bourgeois Virtues* from any standard of cogency.

"I don't much care how 'capitalism' is defined, so long as it is not defined a priori to mean vice incarnate," she explains. In other words, accept that capitalism is not immoral and McCloskey will prove to you that capitalism is not, in fact, immoral—not much of a trick. This statement is made on page two. By page 14, McCloskey is reconsidering: "I mean by capitalism merely private property and free labor without central planning, regulated by rule of law and by ethical consensus." Depending on what she means, exactly, by "ethical consensus," this definition would cover most human societies since the dawn of recorded history, excepting early Christianity, Soviet Russia, Maoist tyrannies and a few utopian fantasies. Three paragraphs later, perhaps realizing that such a wide definition of capitalism hardly calls for a 508-page polemic, McCloskey issues a clarification: "I am going to use the word 'capitalism' here to mean, usually, modern, European-style capitalism." The most important word here is "usually," because, for the remainder of the book, McCloskey's idea of capitalism shifts between a variety of possible definitions.

Thus, before you are out of the first chapter, "loose and baggy" has become lost and batty, a problem that also plagues her treatment of virtue. Part of her muddle arises from her failure to recognize the inherent ambiguity in the idea of virtue itself that dates back to the original Greek conception of arete. McCloskey seems unclear if she means the Platonic, the Aristotelian, or the Christian conception of virtue. She sometimes leans on the idea of virtue as a "habit of the heart" at other times she imagines it as a measurable characteristic of modern society ("love is thicker on the ground in the modern, Western, capitalist world.") The first defines virtue as an internal state, the second as a quantifiable epiphenomenon of open markets.

But any attempt to conflate the various meanings of virtue leads to obvious problems. More wealth does not add up to more generosity, at least if this is defined as a deliberate act of self-sacrifice, and McCloskey's refusal to recognize the difference is maddening. In other words, had the widow in Luke 21:2 invested her two mites in a Roth IRA and donated the dividend, this would seemingly constitute a superior act of virtue for McCloskey. The objection that virtue characterized by self-sacrifice is necessarily elusive in an affluent society seems never to occur to her throughout the expanse of the book and she leaves the issue unaddressed.

The result is a vision of virtue that many will not recognize. McCloskey argues convincingly that a grocer greeting his customers with a friendly "hello" is not necessarily acting out of pure self-interest, but she has not shown how this amounts to love in any recognizable way. What inducements does capitalism offer for the love of the destitute and the ill—meaning not the donation of disposable income to a local charity, but an act of self-sacrifice on their behalf? This objection is not solved by invoking the Aristotelian idea of virtue as habit, as even a habit of spiritless donation fails to amount to charity in the traditional sense of the word.

In more capable hands this would have made an interesting subject of discussion. Unfortunately, McCloskey has dismissed ethical conundrums as "high-school stuff," a judgment she seems to hold for all moral reasoning. The effect is to excuse herself once again from the task of constructing a strong central argument by defining her terms with the necessary exactitude. High school stuff should not be forgotten upon graduation, the reader wants to remind McCloskey, but mastered and built upon. Unfortunately, Deirdre McCloskey has not accomplished either task in this book.

CONTRIBUTORS

Seth Gurgel is the Shanghai Research Fellow for the U.S.-Asia Law Institute, New York School of Law's platform for Asian law and policy study, headed by the accomplished East Asian legal scholar, Professor Jerome Cohen. Seth's areas of research are Chinese Criminal Justice and Labor Law, with a particular interest in rule of law development and Chinese jurisprudence. He is a 2009 graduate of New York University Law School, where he was both a Root-Tilden-Kern Scholar and an Institute for International Law and Justice Fellow. Seth hails from Wisconsin, and is continually surprised at how Midwest American and Chinese self-deprecation complement each other.

Jacob M. Held is assistant professor in the Department of Philosophy and Religion at the University of Central Arkansas. His research interests include nineteenth century German philosophy and political and legal theory with a recent focus on pornography, discrimination, objectification, and free speech.

John J. Liptay, Jr., assistant professor in the Department of Philosophy at St. Thomas More College, University of Saskatchewan, received his doctorate from the University of Toronto. Liptay specializes in Aquinas' ethics, and is interested in the ways Aquinas' thought has been developed and extended. He has co-edited a volume of essays on the thought of Bernard Lonergan, S.J., *The Importance of Insight* (University of Toronto Press, 2007).

Harold Anthony Lloyd received his A.B. in Philosophy from Davidson College and his J.D. from Duke University. He currently teaches as an adjunct professor at Wake Forest University School of Law where his courses include classical rhetoric for lawyers, legal writing and commercial lease negotiation. In addition to his legal interests and articles, Prof. Lloyd is a poet and translator whose translations include *The Complete Epigrams of Palladas,* Racine's *Phèdre,* and Molière's *Tartuffe*.

Yunus Tuncel received his Ph.D. in philosophy in 2000 from the New School for Social Research and has been teaching at Pace University as an adjunct faculty member since then. He is one of the co-founders of the Nietzsche Circle based in New York City and serves on its Board of Directors and on the Editorial Board of its electronic journal, *The Agonist*. His areas of research are art, culture, myth, and spectacle. His book, *Towards a Genealogy of Spectacle*, was published by Eye Corner Press in March 2011.

For more information on Pace titles, please visit the website:
http://www.pace.edu/press

Please inquire about the availability of back issues published prior to 2000 (listed below) at Paceupress@gmail.com

1982 Vol. III, No. 2 **Reason in the Natural Law**

1986 Vol. VI, No. 1 **Edmund Burke and the Natural Law: Theory and Practice**
No. 2 **Is There a Natural Law in Hebrew Tradition?**

1987 Vol. VII, No. 1 **Natural Law and Constitutionalism**
No. 2 **Natural Law and Constitutionalism II**

1988 Vol. VIII, No. 1 **Rights I**
No. 2 **Rights II**

1989 Vol. IX, No. 1 **(General Interest)**
No. 2 **The Spanish Tradition** (Index: Yves R. Simon)

1990 Vol. X, No. 1 **Thomas Aquinas**
No. 2 **(General Interest)**

1991 Vol. XI, No. 1 **Equity as Natural Law**
No. 2 **Sacred and Secular Natural Law**

1992 Vol. XII, No. 1 **Jurisprudence and the Natural Law**
No. 2 **Legal Positivism, Pragmatism**

1993 Vol. XIII, **Dignity as Natural Law**
Nos. 1 & 2 (double issue) (Rosmini, Trigeaud)

1994 Vol. XIV, **Empirical Natural Law, Human Nature, Science**
Nos. 1 & 2 (double issue)

1995 Vol. XV, **Autonomy, Independence, Liberty**
Nos. 1 & 2 (double issue) (Includes 6-year cumulative index: 1990–1995)

2000 New Series Vol. I **Natural Law and Natural Environment**
Nos. 1 & 2 (double issue) (available direct from Pace UP)

2001 New Series Vol. II **Liberalism and Natural Law**
Nos. 1 & 2 (double issue) (available direct from Pace UP)

2002 New Series Vol. III **Globalism and Natural Law**
Nos. 1 & 2 (double issue) (available direct from Pace UP)

2003 New Series Vol. IV **Feminism and Natural Law**
Nos. 1 & 2 (double issue) (available direct from Pace UP)

2004 New Series Vol. V **Medieval Natural Law Theories**
Nos. 1 & 2 (double issue) (available direct from Pace UP)

2005 New Series Vol. VI **The Work of John Finnis**
Nos. 1 & 2 (double issue) (available direct from Pace UP)

2006 New Series Vol. VII **Natural Law Theory & Asian Thought**
Nos. 1 & 2 (double issue) (available direct from Pace UP)

2007 New Series Vol. VIII **(General Interest)**
Nos. 1 & 2 (double issue) (available direct from Pace UP)

2008 New Series Vol. IX **(Virginia Black)**
Nos. 1 & 2 (double issue) (available direct from Pace UP)

2009 New Series Vol. X **(Moral issues)**
Nos. 1 & 2 (double issue) (available direct from Pace UP)

www.ingramcontent.com/pod-product-compliance
Lightning Source LLC
Chambersburg PA
CBHW061451300426
44114CB00014B/1926